"Talking for a Purpose"

Language to Increase Compliance

Say What You Mean and Mean What You Say

MS. MORRISH (MSc)

Independent Behaviour Consultant

Founder of Change Behaviour

Empowering Teachers, Parents and Children

Ms. Morrish (MSc)

First Edition Published by MS. MORRISH (MSc)

Copyright © 2020 MS. MORRISH (MSc)

WOW Book Publishing™

All rights reserved. Neither this book, nor any parts within it may be sold or reproduced in any form without permission.

No part of this book may be reproduced in any form or by any electronic or mechanical means including information storage and retrieval systems, without permission in writing from the author. The only exception is by a reviewer, who may quote short excerpts in a review.

The views and opinions expressed in this book are that of the author based on her personal experiences and education. The author does not guarantee that anyone following the techniques, suggestions, ideas or strategies will become successful.

The author shall neither be liable nor responsible for any loss or damage allegedly arising from any information or suggestion in this book.

"Talking for a Purpose"

| DEDICATION |

I wrote this book for all adults who work within education. This book was written so that you, as the reader, will be empowered to make positive choices around your behaviour. To take ownership of your language and responses, when managing any classroom challenges.

I dedicate this book to my mum, Larraine, who has spent unlimited hours listening and believing in my concepts, when no one else would.

Also, for every single educator who has listened to and then implemented *"Talking for a Purpose"* worldwide.

Respect,

MS. MORRISH (MSc)

Independent Behaviour Consultant

Ms. Morrish (MSc)

|Testimonial|

"Ms Morrish has achieved what she was employed to achieve. Her behaviour approaches have made a huge difference to children's behaviour and has earned the loyalty of both teachers and pupils.

If I was a head teacher today, then this is a model I would seriously consider, and Ms Morrish a consultant whose expertise and opinions I would take very seriously.

If a school is struggling to manage behaviour, Ms Morrish is the first person I would call upon."

Mr Ian Morton

Interim Education Board

Ms. Morrish (MSc)

Acknowledgments

Thank you, to you the reader for reading this book. I very much appreciate it. I truly believe that this book will support you within your classroom setting. I would also like to thank my proof readers, the amazing head teacher Mrs Burrell and my best friend for over twenty years, Lisa Walker. Your honest and structured feedback has helped to shape the book as it is today.

To everyone who has made a comment on a social media post, a private message and the phone calls. Your words of encouragement have meant more than you would ever know.

To Dr Sonia Burnard for mentoring and challenging me to think differently throughout my career. The teacher training colleges that I lecture for, who firmly believe in the positive impact that this approach has upon the classroom behaviour, of both the children and all adults. Also, thank you to the many schools that have consistently embedded my ethos, values and vision and continue to do so, with successful implementation.

Finally, Jenny Oakley who was the one who has made me write this book. Jenny was the only person who had the guts to tell me that I was being selfish in not sharing my concepts and philosophies.

I thank you all……

Ms. Morrish (MSc)

"Talking for a Purpose"

| FOREWORD |

The importance of managing the complexities of the classroom both academic and the learning behaviour is a key professional issue in the training of teachers and in their ongoing practice. This book focuses on the adults in the classroom, the importance of their language and their understanding of the impact of their own behaviour on the world of the classroom.

Ms. Morrish brings her own reflections of her childhood, poignantly sharing the obstacles she faced and the behaviour she exhibited as a basis to her determination to improve the ethos of the classroom both for future adults and the children.

As she says, *"I really liked school but school didn't always like me."* The understanding of her trials and some tribulations she faced in primary and secondary school influences, in part, her successful approach in the training of initial teacher training and the supporting of practicing teachers.

She comments: "Upon reflection and looking back at both my primary and secondary school experiences, I am genuinely thankful for what I had experienced within my schooling. Some of the more positive aspects have most definitely stayed with me and the not-so-positive aspects have definitely helped shape my views around behaviour."

Ms. Morrish (MSc)

She was influenced by her mentors, early in her career, of the importance of the adults' behaviour and language in the classroom as key to managing the varied learning behaviour of the children. She also reflected on why, one teacher in particular was successful in his classroom management, "Not only was he consistent with his expectations, it was very clear to us all that there was a time for some jokes and a time for work, portrayed primarily through his effective use of language."

Ms. Morrish feels that is important for teachers to "say what they mean and mean what they say". Chapters on ways of using effective language in the classroom and what is ineffective language will make the reader think about their own practice. Perhaps not popular initially with teachers is the idea that it is not just the behaviour of the children that may have to be positively developed but also the behaviour of the adults. Again, Ms. Morrish reflects on her experience in school, "Upon reflection, it was not the subject that made an impact and a significant difference to my behaviour — it was the teachers' behaviour."

This book encourages and motivates readers to change their own modes of teaching and to personally learn new skills in managing their own personal language and behaviour that will improve their management of the learning environment. It is about looking at own behaviour which is key to helping teachers to be confident, authoritative.

This is a very practical book and one which all teachers and other professional readers can benefit from. The language used is clear and concise. Ms. Morrish comments that *"I have spent my whole life since secondary school working in different educational capacities.*

"Talking for a Purpose"

I was passionate, adamant and determined to create an ethos and a model that could be replicated throughout schools that actually focuses upon adults' behaviour." On reflection she shares, *"Looking back, I wish that some of my teachers had received "Talking for a Purpose" training. I may have been more compliant. I may have been more focused. I may have completed more tasks."*

Fullan, M., Hargreaves, A., (1996) talk about the effective implementation of educational change consisting of successful teacher development and alterations in curriculum materials, instructional practices and behaviour and beliefs and understandings on the part of teachers involved in innovations.

In fact, specifically Ms. Morrish has brought change to teacher practice in many schools through her training outlined in this book. She has supported teachers in understanding the new practice and this has underpinned the successful practice of managing teaching and learning behaviour within whole schools.

As one head teacher stated, *"We have implemented "Talking for a Purpose" within our school for the past nine years. Due to the consistency of the adult's language, "Talking for a Purpose" provides time and recognition that creates a platform for the development of positive relationships between ALL adults and ALL children."*

You will find that you will be engaged as you now start reading this engaging discourse with consistently instructive commentaries and relevant activities.

Dr Sonia Burnard

Education Consultant

Ms. Morrish (MSc)

"Talking for a Purpose"

|Contents|

|Dedication| 3
|Testimonial| 5
|Acknowledgments| 7
|Foreword| 9
|Contents| 13
|Dear Reader| 15
Why did I write this book? 15
|CHAPTER ONE| 17
Primary School Experiences 17
|CHAPTER TWO| 21
Secondary School Experiences 21
|CHAPTER THREE| 33
The Beginning – Jack 33
|CHAPTER FOUR| 37
Baltimore Bound 37
|CHAPTER FIVE| 47
Are Teachers Leaving the Profession due to Poor Classroom Behaviour? 47
|CHAPTER SIX| 55
Identifying Your Behaviour Button 55
|CHAPTER SEVEN| 61

'Initial' and 'Secondary' Responses 61
|CHAPTER EIGHT| 73
The Managing State Model (MSM) - Managing Your 'Heightened State' 73
|CHAPTER NINE| 87
Redundant Questions 87
Redundant Statement 98
|CHAPTER TEN| 103
Exact Moment Behaviour (EMB) 103
|CHAPTER ELEVEN| 119
The Drop And Stretch Technique 119
|CHAPTER TWELVE| 127
The Impact of Changing Key Words for a Positive Behavioural Outcome 127
|CHAPTER THIRTEEEN| 141
Choosing not to Attend 141
|CHAPTER FOURTEEN| 151
The Effective Commands Model 151
|CONCLUSION| 171
|Me, in my oversized school blazer| 173
|Feedback| 175
|INDEX| 179
|Book References| 181

|DEAR READER|

Why did I write this book?

My behaviour at school was not always the best. However, in my opinion, neither was the behaviour of some of my teachers. I was quickly labelled as a troublemaker and, at times, a 'difficult to manage student.' I was often in detention where my 'punishment' was to write out and copy a page from the telephone directory.

This disciplinary action in no way helped me positively change my behaviour. In fact, I quite liked detention, especially on a cold day. I got to see my friends, write a few lines and keep warm. All the while, there was a teacher at the front of the room, not engaging with any of us. It was as if we were not even there.

Regarding both my primary and secondary schooling, I can name many, many teachers that just could not control the class and could not manage, not just my behaviour but the behaviour of my peers. Many of my teachers appeared disengaged with teaching and just did not appear as though they wanted to educate us.

Several teachers would just ask me to leave the classroom, even when I felt I was complying with class requirements. I questioned why these adults had made the conscious decision to become educators.

Ms. Morrish (MSc)

I often wondered what it was that initially motivated these individuals to choose education as their profession. Yet, now, after working for over twenty-five years with thousands of educators, my perspective has changed. My question now, instead of why they chose to be educators, has shifted to how prepared were they to understand not only basic classroom management principles, but much more importantly, how their language, responses and behaviour has had a direct impact upon every single pupil that they teach.

The purpose of writing this book is so that all people working in the education sector have a clear understanding of the key principles underlying *Talking for a Purpose*. It is about delivering knowledge and skills to successfully implement each of the subsections within educational establishments.

This book has been written with a clear vision to encourage all educators to examine classroom management through an alternative lens. This means changing the focus from children's behaviour and refocusing it on adult behaviour; by empowering all adults to take complete ownership of their behaviour, language and responses within the school setting.

Finally, I simply wanted to write this book so that children are not treated the way that I was treated at school.

| CHAPTER ONE |

Primary School Experiences

"I really liked school but school didn't always like me."

MS. MORRISH (MSc)

Independent Behaviour Consultant

Many people often ask me what I was really like at school. And my answer is always the same. I really liked school but school didn't always like me. I attended a small local primary school with maybe twenty children in my year group. What I remember really distinctly about my primary school is that I was only one of four girls.

I remember going through school thinking we were quite unique and super cool. Although we were all cool, one noticeable difference was the other three girls in my class were really academically 'smart'. I realised from a very young age, maybe five or six, that I was not quite on their level.

How did I know? I was never put in any academic sets for work or tables for children who needed to be 'challenged' academically. I struggled to access a lot of the curriculum. I did not fully understand what was being asked of me.

Ms. Morrish (MSc)

Even from a young age, the one thing that I have always been good at is sports. Give me a ball, racket or a target and I am first in line. My proudest primary school moment, without a doubt, was that I was the FIRST girl EVER to be selected to play in a boys' football team. I was only allowed one game as girls and boys under fourteen were not allowed to play against each other.

I knew this and played my heart out. I scored a goal and I could not believe it. I thought I was the champion of the world. I remember floating on air as I walked home to tell my parents. However, when I got back to the classroom the next day, I thought everyone would be talking about the team's win and my goal. Instead, we had a math test.

I struggled to maintain my attention. I failed miserably. I can clearly remember sitting in my chair thinking, I am the only girl that scored a goal in football in the whole history of this primary school, yet I cannot add up these numbers. The goal, of course, had been quickly forgotten.

Around the age of ten, we had to complete standardised academic tasks. I can still vividly remember the timetables being displayed, on large pieces of paper throughout the classroom. My teacher was great, I loved him; I thought he was funny and engaging. But I just could not complete the task like everyone else. He recognised this and he approached my mum.

My mother was a teacher with over thirty years of teaching experience. She would come into school and he would talk to her, and my mum did absolutely everything to support me at home, but I just did not always understand what was being asked of me.

At this primary school they used a house point system. Every term we were acknowledged for what we had achieved. There were lots of prizes such as bookmarks, pens, vouchers, yet all of these were for 'academic achievement'.

So, I set myself a challenge by the end of the school year, I was going to achieve an academic acknowledgement. So, I asked for extra help. My teacher was supportive and worked with my mum and then we worked together at home, consistently.

At the end of the autumn term, numerous children received prizes for increasing in their abilities within numeracy or literacy. I got the most helpful classmate. That's OK, I thought to myself. I worked my hardest, and again, I got the most helpful person in the classroom the following term. For the last term, as I was about to start secondary school, I really needed to focus, work hard, and concentrate in class.

I believed in myself, I knew I could do it! My name got called out for the most helpful person in the classroom despite everything that I had done to support my own academic progress and the level of being disheartened at the age of 11 was huge.

Now, I realise that I was not completing much work. I just was not on the same level as everyone else. I was probably a bit too active, easily distracted and inattentive. However, it was not until I got to secondary school, that my behaviour started to change.

Ms. Morrish (MSc)

Reflective Questions:

1. What were your primary school experiences like?

   _____

   _____

2. Did your school have a behaviour system/approach?

   _____

   _____

   _____

3. If yes, was it effective? And why do you think it was/ wasn't effective?

   _____

|CHAPTER TWO|

SECONDARY SCHOOL EXPERIENCES

My first real memory of starting my secondary schooling was the excitement about my school uniform. I really liked the colours—black and purple and I just could not wait to get my blazer on. I can remember my mum taking me to the official school shop, and I kept saying, *"This blazer doesn't fit, it doesn't fit"*. To this day, I still do not know whether she gave me my brother's hand-me-down blazer and told me that I was going to grow into it over the next three years.

I went to secondary school, in my really oversized blazer. I remember the first thing we had to do was sit in, what felt like the biggest school hall ever made. It felt really huge coming from a small primary school. I sat down alongside two of the girls from my primary school. Then the teachers entered, who all walked in a silent line, then sat on chairs on the stage of the huge hall. One by one, each teacher stood up, walked to the front of the stage and started to read aloud random names.

My two friends were both called in the first group. I happily sat there in my oversized blazer confidently assuming that the teacher had just missed my name off the list and I would soon be reunited with my two, primary school friends. I waited, and I waited, and I waited until there were about thirty children remaining out of what seemed like thousands.

Ms. Morrish (MSc)

Everyone sat sporadically in the biggest school hall ever made. Then finally a sigh of relief as my name was called-incorrectly, but called nonetheless. My heart sank when I realised that I had been placed in the second from bottom academic class in the whole year group.

I felt embarrassed and a little ashamed. Is this the class for the 'thickos'? I happily skipped to find my friends at playtime. They asked what class I was now in and when I told them they looked uncomfortable and embarrassed. I realised my football goal was now completely forgotten and I never really spoke to my primary school friends again. I decided to stay determined through my first year of secondary school by working hard in all my subjects.

Yet, there were many teachers who really had a limited interest in teaching us. Due to my inability to maintain focus and attention, I got bored very quickly. I did not feel supported by some teachers and with no clear expectations or boundaries, I thought I could push a few buttons. Some teachers had commented to me about how disruptive I had become. I explained that I was bored in lessons. This was then perceived as me being difficult and disrespectful. On entering my second year at secondary school, I decided that I was going to live up to the label.

Living Up to the Label

'I am going to make myself harder for you to teach.' I became disruptive. I removed myself from classes. By the age of thirteen, I was locking teachers up in cupboards. I remember being part of a

group that set a fire alarm off on numerous occasions. I also let the air out of the tires of some teachers' cars and there was not really much point in following instructions.

I can recall being in science class, and setting off the Bunsen burners and dancing with the skeleton in the room. The teacher just could not manage the class and often looked like he was going to cry. The mission was to make him cry. Mission accepted and completed numerous times. However, having a disruptive label also had another aspect. I was often accused of things that I truthfully did not do.

One such incident was, of all things, eggs. I was thirteen, and one of my teachers accused me of stealing eggs out of her home economics room. I was reprimanded, severely and publicly, in front of all my classmates. No matter how much I tried to explain that it was not me, I was told that I was an extremely rude and inconsiderate child.

It was not until I got home and showed my mum the detention slip and I said, *"Yet again, I am the one that's been treated unfairly."* I was not even in school that day due to a hospital appointment. Interestingly, I was never considered a 'problem' at home. Even though I may be biased, I consider my parents to be the best in the world.

They have raised me to be determined, resilient and confident. What they also instilled in me was accountability. I knew that I needed to change my behaviour and be more accountable. I started to associate with different friends, focus more on my school work and completed homework. I attended extra study sessions and stayed out of detention. I increased my own accountability of my actions. It was nearly the end of the second year of my GCSEs and I was finally, believing again.

I was now not the child wearing an oversized blazer waiting and waiting for her name to be called. I was going to prove them wrong. I was going to follow in my mother's footsteps. I was going to change the education system. I was going to change classrooms. I was going to change how teachers teach children. I was going to be a teacher! I am ready for my GSCEs and my A Levels. Who would have thought; me as a teacher?

Labelled as Educationally Subnormal

I was sent to my Head of Year's office. I was fifteen years old and in the second year of completing my GCSEs. I felt that I had worked extremely hard at turning my behaviour around. Once I sat down in the Head of Year's office, I explained that I would like to do my A-levels at school as I wanted to be a teacher.

I sat there so proud. To this day, I am not sure if he laughed out loud so loudly because he was shocked or because he thought I was joking. I said again, very clearly, *"Sir, I think I would make a really good teacher."* He stared straight at me and said, *"You do realise that you are educationally subnormal? There is never going to be a possibility that you complete or even apply to do your A-levels at this school. What I suggest you do is go to the school up the road and do drama; because that's obviously where your strength lies in being able to perform in front of an audience."*

Those words still play out in my head to this day. I was devastated. I had done what had been asked of me at school and it still was not considered enough. I wonder if this adult ever stopped to think of the impact that his words and language had on my behaviour. Today I am a conference presenter and the behaviour management lecturer for teacher training colleges. I deliver INSET sessions on the topics of behaviour and classroom management, throughout the country; and yes, I am most definitely a performer.

My Personal Insight into Education

Upon reflection and looking back at both my primary and secondary school experiences, I am genuinely thankful for what I had experienced within my schooling. Some of the more positive aspects have most definitely stayed with me and the not-so-positive aspects have definitely helped shape my views around behaviour.

I have spent my whole life since secondary school working in different educational capacities. I was passionate, adamant and determined to create an ethos and a model that could be replicated throughout schools that actually focused upon adults' behaviour.

Looking back, I wish that some of my teachers had received *"Talking for a Purpose"* training. I may have been more compliant. I may have been more focused. I may have completed more tasks. I may have actually passed more than two GCSEs. I may not have been labelled as being so disruptive.

Ms. Morrish (MSc)

I may not have answered back to the hundred and one redundant questions that were asked throughout the day. I may have been able to maintain my focus, and I may have been in a much better position to accept the positive comments that were said to me, instead of living within a self-fulfilling prophecy that I am academically never going to be successful.

Words are Powerful

The labels which teachers give to pupils can influence the construction and development of children's identities, or self-concepts: how they see and define themselves and how they interact with peers and adults. This in turn, can affect their attitudes towards school, their behaviour, and ultimately their level of achievement in education.

According to labelling theory (Becker, H, 1963) teachers actively judge their pupils over a period of time, making judgements based on their behaviour in class, attitude to learning, previous school reports and interactions with them and their parents. This eventually classifies their students according to whether they are 'high' or 'low' ability, 'hard working' or 'lazy', 'naughty' or 'well-behaved', 'in need of support' or 'capable of just getting on with it'.

A closely related concept to labelling theory is that of the self-fulfilling prophecy, where an individual accepts their label and the label becomes true in practice, for example, a student labelled as deviant actually becomes deviant as a response to being labelled as one.

Classic Studies on Teacher Labelling in Education

Most of the work of labelling theory applied to education was done in the late 1960s and early 1970s. Four classic works, summarised below include:

- David Hargreaves (1975) Deviance in Classrooms
- R.C. Rist (1970) Student Social Class and Teachers' Expectations: The Self-Fulfilling Prophecy of Ghetto Education
- Rosenthal and Jacobson (1968) Pygmalion in the Classroom
- Margaret Fuller's (1984) research on black girls in a London comprehensive school

Labelling Theory and the Self-Fulfilling Prophecy

Self-Fulling Prophecy Theory argues that predictions made by teachers about the future success or failure of a student have a tendency to become true, because that prediction has been made. Therefore, if a student is labelled a success, they will succeed, if they are labelled a failure, they will fail.

A classic study which supports the self-fulfilling prophecy theory was Rosenthal and Jacobson's (1968) study of an elementary school in California. They selected a random sample of 20% of the student population and informed teachers that these students could be expected to achieve rapid intellectual development.

They tested all students at the beginning of the experiment for IQ, and again after one year, and found that the randomly selected 'spurter' group had, on average, gained more IQ than the other 80%, who the teachers believed to be 'average'.

They also found that the report cards for the 20% group showed that the teachers believed this group had made greater advances in reading. Rosenthal and Jacobson (1968) speculated that the teachers had passed on their higher expectations to students which had produced a self-fulfilling prophecy.

However, negative labelling can sometimes have the opposite effect. Margaret Fuller's (1984) research on black girls in a London comprehensive school found that the black girls she researched were labelled as low-achievers, but their response to this negative labelling was to knuckle down and study hard to prove their teachers and the school wrong.

Waterhouse (2004), in case studies of four primary and secondary schools, suggests that teacher-labelling of pupils as either normal/average or deviant, as a result of impressions formed over time, has implications for the way teachers interact with pupils.

Once these labels are applied and become the dominant categories for pupils, they can become what Waterhouse (2004) called a 'pivotal identity' for students—a core identity providing a pivot which teachers use to interpret and reinterpret classroom events and student behaviour.

For example, a student who has the pivotal identity of 'normal' is likely to have an episode of deviant behaviour interpreted as unusual, or as a 'temporary phase'—something which will shortly end, thus requiring no significant action to be taken; whereas a student who has a pivotal identity of 'deviant' will have periods of 'good behaviour' treated as unusual, something which is not expected to last, and thus not worthy of recognition.

Reflective task:

Take a moment to reminisce about your own school experiences. I am sure you can remember a teacher that really inspired you. This teacher kept you engaged in lessons and supported you with your learning.

Perhaps the teacher that you are currently thinking of was funny, yet fair and consistent in their approach to classroom management and had a clear understanding of their own values and beliefs on teaching. I also was lucky enough to be taught by some outstanding teachers.

Upon reflection, it was not the subject that made an impact and a significant difference to my behaviour—it was the teachers' behaviour. I took history GCSE only because I was told that I had to by the Head of Year, as he did not want me disrupting other classes. Now, at the time I had no interest in history as a subject at all. Yet from the first lesson I was engaged. So, what made the difference? From the first moment we were all in the class, it was clearly explained to us what the teacher's expectations of us were as well as his expectations for his students.

He was clear and precise in his words, explained the positive outcomes and highlighted the negative consequences of our decisions. When we were given assignments, there was not a 'one

Ms. Morrish (MSc)

rule fits all' approach. He let us take responsibility for our own learning as long as we discovered the main objectives. Then on a personal note, one of the most significant aspects was that it was hands-on learning.

What I remember most was his approach to classroom management. Not only was he consistent with his expectations, it was very clear to us all that there was a time for some jokes and a time for work, portrayed primarily through his effective use of language.

Reflective Questions and Activities:

Think about a teacher that really inspired you.

1. What was it about this teacher that you remember most?

   _____

2. Write down all the words that come to mind when thinking about this teacher.

   _____

   _____

"Talking for a Purpose"

3. Think about a teacher that you did not like at school. What was it about this teacher that you disliked?

_____

_____

_____

4. Write down all the words that come to mind when thinking about this teacher.

_____

_____

5. How has your school experiences shaped your views regarding classroom management?

_____

Ms. Morrish (MSc)

|CHAPTER THREE|

The Beginning – Jack

From 2001 to 2004, I worked for a company that specialised in early identification and early intervention for preschool children with a range of identified special educational needs. The company consisted of a team of Key Workers and Specialist Teachers who worked together to support families within the home and preschool setting.

As a Key Worker, I worked with several families, yet one played a crucial part in the process of developing *"Talking for a Purpose"*. I was the Key Worker for a pre-schooler named Jack and his mother. Before taking on this role, I had already spent over ten years working in various educational settings including a residential school for children excluded from their primary schools. I considered myself skilled at managing challenging behaviours.

To be honest, as I was driving to meet Jack and his mother for my introductory visit, my thought was, *"This child is a pre-schooler, how hard can it be?"* I went to the visit with my 'behaviour toolkit' consisting of various enticing and exciting toys to support Jack to follow instructions.

Ms. Morrish (MSc)

I had also been acknowledged from previous supervisors in my ability to develop positive relationships with parents and carers. I thought that I was going to walk in and build a rapport with his mother relatively quickly. Well, it was a very different story when I actually got there. She was extremely difficult to engage with, was negative in her views around support and talked about 'fixing him'.

Any suggestions that I initially came up with, she would not attend to or participate in. I would spend hours modelling some basic behaviour management techniques for her. I explained the significance of positive rewards and also consequences. I talked about the importance of routines and boundaries. I emphasised the significance of consistency.

I developed visual supports and an individual reward system for Jack. Her response was consistently the same. *"I've already done it. I've had fifteen professional people in here already telling me the same thing. Nothing works, he just doesn't listen."* No matter how hard I tried, I was just unable to find a way to develop a relationship with the parent. After spending several weeks of trying to figure out a way to develop a positive rapport with Jack's mother, I made a crucial decision.

I decided to put away all the enticing toys, routine rule book and visual supports that I had made and focus purely on her and not on Jack. I spent more time listening than speaking. A key feature I observed and reflected on was how vocal this parent was. She would not necessarily get up and move. She would not really engage in the offered activities, but she was very, very vocal.

Now what I mean by vocal is she spoke A LOT; and every time I thought, what would happen if I changed her language? What would happen if I modified the way she spoke to Jack? Would that make a significant difference regarding his behaviour?

I decided to work with what I had found was a strong characteristic of the mother and that was how she spoke: the words she used. For the next year, twice a week, I worked with her specifically on how she was giving instructions to Jack. We discussed how many words we thought Jack was not only hearing yet also understanding. Together, we identified key behavioural words and phrases. I identified an optimal tone range for her, which we practiced on each and every visit.

Mum started to engage and Jack listened and started to become much more compliant. I then supported the teaching staff within Jack's pre-school to implement the same key words and phrases and emphasised the significance of consistent language with any additional supports. Jack's behaviour significantly improved both within pre-school and at home. After two years of working with Jack and his mother, it was time for me to say goodbye as their Key Worker.

This time was different. My final visit involved a coffee with mum and a chat that didn't focus on Jack's behaviour. There was one sentence that will always stay with me. As I was leaving, Jack's mum said, *"Thank you, I feel like I can now enjoy my son."*

Ms. Morrish (MSc)

|CHAPTER FOUR|

Baltimore Bound

"The question is not is Ms. Morrish ready for Baltimore. The real question is Baltimore ready for her?"

Gemma Butler,

Special Educational Needs Specialist; UK

In 2004 I was offered a truly unique opportunity. However, this opportunity entailed making a huge life-changing decision of leaving the UK and moving alone to the east coast of America. I was to be employed by the University of Maryland, Baltimore and was going to be a member of a clinical team consisting of social workers, child psychiatrists, and trauma therapists, from the Centre of Infant study.

I have never been a person to shy away from a challenge, so I grabbed this opportunity with both hands. I thought, *"I have been to America a few times. This will be like an extended holiday."* I did not

Ms. Morrish (MSc)

actually do any research on Baltimore and there is still a part of me today that is glad that I didn't. To say it was a complete culture shock would be a massive understatement. One thing that was apparent straight away was that this experience was most certainly NOT going to be a holiday.

Baltimore, USA

Steeped in history, Baltimore is the site of the first casualty in the American Civil War, the birthplace of the American national anthem, a city of sport lovers who bleed purple (Baltimore Ravens-American Football) and orange (Orioles—Baseball), a city of Edgar Allen Poe and David Simon, and a distinct personality like no other city in the United States.

It has a lot more to offer than what is shown in the two gripping TV dramas: Life on the Street and The Wire. The 'Charm City' lies about 35 miles from Washington D.C., at the western arm of the Chesapeake Bay along the east coast of the United States and is the largest city in Maryland state. Famous Baltimore natives are Barry Levinson, Ogden Nash, Henry Louis Mencken, Frederick Douglass, Babe Ruth, Cal Ripken, Billie Holiday, Edith Hamilton, Michael Phelps, and John Waters—the city's equivalent to New York's Woody Allen.

I got introduced quickly to the Baltimorean favourites of steamed blue crabs seasoned with Old Bay and pit beef sandwiches complemented with a cold Natty Boh. Then the amazing Baltimore harbour with the famous Baltimore aquarium. Yet, Baltimore also had:

Baltimore (2018) according to the source, www.areavibes.com

- Baltimore crime rates are 145% higher than the national average
- Violent crimes in Baltimore are 382% higher than the national average
- In Baltimore you have a 1 in 16 chance of becoming a victim of crime
- Baltimore is safer than only 2% of the cities in the United States

My primary employment was to work in a large inner-city school, where I would support families, deliver an evidence-based social skills curriculum, run parent Coffee Hours and deliver workshops on children's development. As I was in a school daily, I had the opportunity to support teaching staff within the classrooms. I had acquired so much experience in the UK, that I was excited to share my knowledge with my new American colleagues. However, my knowledge was not able to be shared for quite some time as I was met with quite a degree of hostility.

Teachers did not want me in their classrooms and did not hold back at all in telling me so. The approach that my predecessors implemented was allowing teaching staff to remove children from the learning environment to then sit, work or play with the specialist. From accounts from the teaching staff, those children were eventually returned to class with stickers and/or candy as they 'had worked well' during their time out of class.

Not Home Until Christmas

I tried to speak to the teaching staff and was simply ignored. I even tried to pull out the old 'British card' and talk about the Queen, nothing. I was told not to come into some classrooms. I was given jobs that had nothing to do with my role. When I first met with the teachers at a group, they asked me how long I planned on being there as most specialists did not last.

They explained that they had specialists before and that it was all a waste of time, and then asked me how I would be any different. I got quizzed on Black History. I survived my first week. I was in inner city Baltimore, alone in an apartment, not even knowing where I actually lived. No friends, no car, no phone and no internet. There was only one thing to do. The one thing I had been holding off doing every single night. I called my parents.

When my mum answered the phone, my heart imploded. My first thought immediately was to ask for a plane ticket home. I desperately wanted to get on a plane, see my family and all my UK friends. Instead, I took a big deep breath and said, *"Even if I ask, do not let me come home till Christmas. Even if I beg and plead, don't let me come home. I need to give myself six months. If they are still not talking to me by Christmas, I will come home."*

"Talking for a Purpose"

My mum, Larraine was as straight talking as ever, said, *"You made the decision to go to Baltimore. You have never given up on anything. If anyone can support this school, it's you. And no, you are not coming home till Christmas."*

By Monday morning, I entered the school with a plan. I had identified three aspects of this school that I felt needed addressing immediately:

1. The number of children who were just sent randomly, with little or no explanation, queuing up outside my office, for me to 'deal with.'

2. The number of children out of class, standing in the corridors, waiting to be told when to re-enter the classroom.

3. Adults vocal volume when speaking to each other and children.

For the first few months, I was not popular at all with any of the teaching staff. Each time a child was sent to me, I took the child immediately back to their classroom. Some teachers then sent the same child back to my office and I again took the child back to the classroom. There were times when I had a queue of children outside my office asking to play games with me.

I told them in no uncertain terms that I did not 'play games' and took each and every child back to their classroom. Each time I returned with a child the teacher would give me a look. Every time I would state, *"Whatever issues you are experiencing are within YOUR classroom. Therefore, the management of behaviour needs to be in class, not my office or the corridors."* I would then disengage and walk away.

Ms. Morrish (MSc)

I would repeat the same sentence in the same way each and every time I returned a child. As time went on, children were still being sent to me. When returning a child now, I would say, *"I can show you how to manage these behaviours so that they can stay in class. You will also have more teaching time."* I said the same sentence in the same way every time.

This interaction went on for many, many weeks. Then finally, a teacher approached me for support. Upon entering the classroom, the teacher explained to me about the disruptive behaviour of a few children. She explained that one child in particular was extremely challenging. She stated that he never listens, calls out, does not follow instructions, can be aggressive and the list went on and on.

I asked her, *"What is the one behaviour that truly plucks your last nerve?"* She looked at me a little bewildered, thought for a moment, then said *"That he never follows any instructions"*. In my mind I thought 'never', yet I kept that thought to myself. I stayed in the class for about forty-five minutes. During that time the teacher asked me on numerous occasions if I was going to 'deal with him'. When I said 'No' she asked bluntly, *"What is the point in you even being there?"* I said, *"Well, you don't know my approach yet."*

My philosophy regarding behaviour started early in my career. I had always been fascinated by human interactions and particularly language. My concepts were first planted around the age of twenty-one. This was a pinnacle time in my life as I met and worked alongside Doctor Sonia Burnard, a Doctor in Education and the director of an established Teacher Training College, with a particular focus upon adults' behaviour within schools. I was totally fascinated with her work, and she instilled in me the importance of adult behaviour and language. This initial plantation continues to grow and flourish every day as I teach the same philosophy to thousands of educators every year.

The children went to lunch and I sat with the teacher and explained my personal philosophies regarding classroom management. That it is the adult's behaviour that needs to be observed and modified before even attempting to manage a child's behaviour.

I explained my rationale by stating that, *"The only thing that you have complete and 100% ownership over, is you."* I then went on to explain that, *"Much of the focus in classrooms is on the behaviour of the children. My focus is 100% adult-driven. This means I don't work with the children. I work with you to support YOU first and foremost so that YOU have the skills to manage children's behaviour, in the classroom."* The teacher said.

"Okay, how do I do it?" It took about five months, but I was in! I thought, well if I can change Jack's mum's behaviour, why not this teacher? So, where did I start?

Her own behaviour and language…

I was initially contracted to work in Baltimore for a year, but I stayed for six. In that time, I was privileged to work with some of the most amazing educators and parents. Once the teaching staff experienced the impact of my approach, they were extremely supportive. The language of adults changed, children's behaviour improved, relationships between adults and children flourished and educators felt empowered.

Ms. Morrish (MSc)

> *"No matter what anybody tells you,*
> *words and ideas can change the world."*
> **John Keating, (1989) Dead Poet's Society**

During a meeting with my supervisor Kay Connors, she asked if I wanted to present the work that I was doing in school at one of the developmental seminars at the University of Maryland. I was thrilled then she asked me the title or name. I instantly replied, *"Name of what?"* Kay looked at me with a clear confusion before she reminded me that I needed a name for my seminars.

I then realised what she meant and before I could think my mouth ran ahead of my mind blurting out, "*Adult language*" thinking yeah, that's a good name. The presentation went well, although in retrospect there was actually only one sub section of *"Talking for a Purpose"* at the time.

The rest was just concepts in my head. I started to write my thoughts down. I drew diagrams and mind maps. I designed charts for teachers and parents to complete. I even made key rings with key phrases on them.

Then I started to record the impact, via teacher interviews and questionnaires. I collected data using the Strength and Difficulties questionnaire, then I ran the stats. With the printout of the stats in my hand, I headed off to meet with one of the main professors within the University of Maryland, Doctor Bruno Anthony.

Doctor Anthony was a leader in the field of Child and Adolescent Psychiatry and extremely well known and well liked, thanks to his approachable manner. I explained my thoughts and findings. After some time, Doctor Anthony said, *"Morrish, I think you may have found something here."* During one of our meetings, I was asked what the title of my work was.

I tried to get away with saying, *"Adult language"*, but this was not accepted. I was then set the task of creating a better name. I returned the following week with a blank piece of A4 paper with the words *"Talking for a Purpose"* Say what you mean and mean what you say, printed in the middle of the paper.

This was the first time I had seen it typed out. I thought to myself, no matter what anyone says, that is the title. Just months before returning to the UK, I was privileged to present the beginnings of *"Talking for a Purpose"* at the same conference as Doctor Anthony on the topic of children's regulation, for the Early Child Mental Health Certificate Program. An experience I will never forget.

"Talking for a Purpose", has now been delivered to thousands of educators and parents throughout the UK. I deliver INSET training to schools. I run *"Talking for a Purpose"* for Parents and Carers groups. I lead *"Talking for a Purpose"* workshops.

I am also the Behaviour Management lecturer for several SCITTS and Teacher Training Colleges for both the primary and secondary education sector. Yet this all started by being given an opportunity to talk about my approach. There are times when what seems like quite a small opportunity actually leads to life-changing events.

So, my advice, big risk = big reward. You never know where it might lead you.

Ms. Morrish (MSc)

|CHAPTER FIVE|

Are Teachers Leaving the Profession due to Poor Classroom Behaviour?

One in four teachers in the UK say they experience physical violence from their pupils at least once a week, and many say poor behaviour is making them want to leave the profession, according to figures compiled by a teaching union.

The NASUWT union found that 24% of the nearly 5,000 teachers who sent in feedback said they were subjected to physical attacks each week. Many reported that they had been 'shoved or barged', and a significant percentage said they had been hit, punched or kicked.

Nearly nine in ten teachers said they had received some sort of verbal or physical abuse from pupils in the past year. 86% said they had been sworn at and 46% said they had been verbally threatened.

Source: The Guardian, April, 2019

Ms. Morrish (MSc)

Three-quarters of teachers frequently have to deal with disruptive behaviour in school and many have considered quitting as a result, a survey has suggested. Almost two-thirds of teachers are considering or have previously thought about leaving the profession, while 71% would-be teachers are being put off by concerns around poor pupil behaviour, the Policy Exchange Think Tank said.

More than half of those asked, said they believed the quality of children's education was affected by disrupted lessons, and 45% said they did not feel their initial training had prepared them to manage pupil behaviour.

Report author Dr Joanna Williams said the findings showed there is an appetite among teachers, parents and students for a tougher approach, but added that rather than bringing in new policies, those already in place need to be more consistently applied.

Among the report's recommendations, the paper entitled 'It Just Grinds You Down', said higher standards of behaviour should be required for schools to achieve good or better Ofsted ratings and that staff should have refreshers in 'Behaviour Management' policies.

Ref: independent paper
December 2018 TES

According to 'Policy Exchange', the findings from the new Deltapoll research include:

- 75% of teachers say they commonly experience disruption in their own school.

- 54% of teachers think the quality of children's education is affected by disrupted lessons.

- 62% of teachers are currently, or have previously, considered leaving the profession because of poor pupil behaviour.

- 71% of the teachers agreed that potential teachers are being put off joining the profession by fear of becoming victim to poor behaviour from pupils.

- 45% of teachers polled claim their initial teacher training did not prepare them to manage pupil behaviour.

Behaviour management is the 'overwhelming problem' faced by trainees who are now entering the classroom sooner and who sometimes find themselves with 'poor quality, inconsistent or entirely absent mentoring', according to ESP ambassador and TES author Emma Kell, who is also head of English at a comprehensive school in North London.

Source TES (Dave Speck July 2019)
(Times Educational Supplement)

Ms. Morrish (MSc)

Exclusions in Numbers

- More than a quarter of permanent exclusions were pupils aged 14—those just about to start their GCSE courses.

- Boys were more than three times as likely as girls to be permanently excluded.

- Pupils claiming free school meals — available to households on lower incomes — were about four times as likely to be excluded.

- Pupils receiving support for special educational needs were the most likely to be excluded (seven times as often as those without special educational needs).

- Black Caribbean pupils were over three times more likely to be permanently excluded than the average.

- Children in the West Midlands are twice as likely to be excluded (12 in every 10,000) as children in the South East of England (six in every 10,000).

Source: Department for Education March 2018

There are many, many aspects that require significant attention to increase positive and pro-social behaviour in schools. At a strategic level, more money for specialist support can be considered, access to better mental health support for children and adults. A general improvement in policy writing can be developed, hands-on coaching for head teachers, increased parental involvement can be encouraged, and all the relevant INSET training on behaviour management can be provided.

Even the implementation of successful behaviour management systems, as well as a better understanding of neurodiversity, and clearer understanding of trauma and attachment theory, consistently implemented routines, effective strategies to encourage and build positive relationships. The list is endless.

Yet, upon consideration, several aspects from the above-mentioned list are possibly out of your control. Therefore, what are you in control of? In fact, right now in this very moment as you read this book, what is the ONLY thing you have control of? The answer is YOU. This book does not examine the requirements behind the education system nationally.

Therefore, the question arises, what can be done to support educators now? I believe the focus of classroom management needs to be shifted so that all educators can take immediate action and ownership regarding their behaviour.

Ms. Morrish (MSc)

Shifting the Focus

'It's funny because I talk about you all the time with parents. I always tell them about how you used to say, "If there is a behaviour issue, I don't even need to see the child. Show me the parent, teacher or adult in their life and I will change the behaviour of the child."

I joke about how I didn't believe you until we started working together! I now use a method that includes parent behaviour modification combined with child focused approaches. All because of you!'

Myque Harris,

LCMHC, RYT—200

I would like you, as the reader, to know that I have a great admiration for those specialists who work within the field of mental health, particularly child and adolescent mental health. Through the years, I have gained significant knowledge with regards to attachment theory and how trauma can often play a significant role in children's challenging behaviours.

I have had the privilege to work alongside some of the most brilliant clinicians, allowing me to learn so much and gain a uniquely different perspective. One such amazing clinician is Myque Harris. After working in Baltimore for about a year, the school-based behavioural and mental health team changed and I began working with Myque, who is a dynamic and energetic psychotherapist, registered yoga teacher, and mindfulness specialist. She truly enjoys working with children, adolescents, and adults.

She supports teens and adults of all ages with identity exploration, anxiety, depression, relationships, and other major life transitions. Her knowledge regarding children's behaviour and mental health is truly outstanding.

One day, we arranged to meet and make plans for the next school term. During this time, we started to discuss behaviour approaches in schools and parent support. It was apparent straight away that we had completely different perspectives. Myque's thoughts were always from the perspective of the child and that the displayed behaviour may possibly be due to an experience.

Also, that the child is communicating via their behaviour and the behaviour has a purpose. I, on the other hand, was primarily only interested in adult behaviour. Essentially being two different approaches, reaching the same goal.

Yet, the core ethos that is throughout *"Talking for a Purpose"* remains the significance of adult's behaviour, language and responses. I believe that it is these elements that are required to be addressed and modified because, to be honest and to reiterate, the only thing you as a teacher have complete 100% ownership over is YOU.

The focus is often upon the behaviour of children, and the adults' behaviour is not always examined. Therefore, shifting the focus will increase each adult's consistency and accountability.

Ms. Morrish (MSc)

*"Talking for a Purpose"*

|CHAPTER SIX|

Identifying Your Behaviour Button

'The first step toward change is awareness'

__Nathaniel Branden (1995)__

By the end of this chapter, you will have a clear understanding of the following:

- ≈ Identification of your personal 'Behaviour Button'.
- ≈ Increased awareness of how you respond when your 'Behaviour Button' is pushed.

I had been in Baltimore for about three months and I was greeting children as they entered school. One boy walked past me with his trousers much lower than his waist. I stopped him and said *"Good morning, what's your name?"* He politely replied, *"My name is Deshawn, ma'am."*

I said, *"Deshawn pull your trousers up, you are now in school."* He looked confused and asked, *"Do you mean my pants?"* Oh, of course being British I meant trousers yet said, *"Yes, pull your pants up and walk into class."* Deshawn pulled his pants up as requested yet as he walked away, he 'sucked his teeth'. The insult that I felt erupted throughout my body. I can clearly remember, it seemed to come from the tips of my toes, through my torso and into my hands.

It felt hot and quick. I had never had anyone suck their teeth at me in the UK. How disrespectful! I am British! So, I literally marched after him and said, *"What did you just do to me?"* He looked at me little bemused by this and explained that he meant no harm or disrespect at all. I immediately felt that I had not managed this situation well at all. I was new in this role and there I was marching after a child because I felt disrespected. What was it that made me respond like that? Was it just a cultural difference?

I soon realised that 'teeth sucking' was not viewed by all in the way that I indeed felt about it. It was explained to me that this was part of the 'Bmore culture'. Not only by children but there were numerous occasions where the parents that I was working with, demonstrated this behaviour.

I found myself responding to this without even thinking about it. I realised for whatever reason, this behaviour was 'pushing my button' to which I was then responding both physiologically and then verbally, usually by asking a question.

Taking ownership of your behaviour starts now. It is time to take ownership of your 'behaviour button'. So, I want to know, what pushes 'your button'? Please note that I ask 'button' and not 'buttons'. It is often easier to write a list of classroom concerns. They will all come flooding out.

One problem or concern leads to another and lists are easy to create. Self-introspection is often uncomfortable. Being uncomfortable is a positive as it often encourages self-reflection and where the accountability for adult behaviour starts. Be uncomfortable. The most productive learning is often not within your own comfort zone.

Behaviour Button activity

You will need a small piece of paper or card.

This activity has three parts:

1. Behaviour identification
2. Personal responses
3. Self-reflection

Part One: Behaviour Identification

Take a moment and think about the ONE behaviour, just the MAIN ONE that absolutely gets on your nerves while you are teaching within your classroom. Please note that this is not a list. Take your time and think about one and only one that totally frustrates you as a teacher. Write it down on the piece of card in front of you. Write the behaviour without an explanation or scenario; just the behaviour.

Then take a moment to immerse yourself back into that situation. Perhaps your 'button' is: being ignored, not being listened to, being interrupted while teaching, children self-exiting the classroom, or the noise level during independent work?

If you are a visual person, picture the incident. If you are an auditory person, hear what was said and how it was said. If you are more of a kinaesthetic person, remember how you felt at this time. Multi-sensory, utilise all of the above modes.

Whatever it is, I want you to write it as clearly as you can on your piece of paper or card. Writing this on your card or paper is vital. We are all used to typing on a computer, laptop or phone, and this information is so easy to delete and edit.

Writing down the ONE behaviour that pushes your 'button' will help take your subconscious thoughts and make it more conscious for you.

Part Two: Personal Responses

Now you have the ONE significant behaviour that really gets on your nerves. Again, take a moment and close your eyes and immerse yourself. Relive your 'button' by seeing, hearing, or feeling, or combining all senses together.

Now take your piece of paper or card that has your most frustrating behaviour on it and turn it over. Then write on the back of the card the answer to this question: How did you respond?

"Talking for a Purpose"

Part three: Self Reflection

What was your response?
_____

Did you state a consequence to the behaviour?
_____

Did you repeat your instruction again?
_____

Did you explain the expectations of the classroom?
_____

Did you explain how this behaviour was not acceptable?
_____

Did you ask the child a question such as why are you still calling out?

Ms. Morrish (MSc)

Did the volume of your words increase?

Also, did you feel your heartbeat increase?

Did you feel a knot in your stomach?

Was there a hot sensation somewhere in your body?

Did you feel any tingling sensations?

| CHAPTER SEVEN |

'Initial' and 'Secondary' Responses

'Between stimulus and response there is a space. In that space is our power to choose our response. In our response lies our growth and our freedom.'

Victor E Frankl

By the end of this chapter, you will have a clear understanding of the following:

- ≈ The term Initial Response
- ≈ The term Secondary Response
- ≈ The significance of practising out of context
- ≈ An example of practising out of context
- ≈ The Cycle of Defiance
- ≈ How to Stop and Think BEFORE you Speak

Also, at the end of the chapter, you will complete a reflective task which will increase your understanding of:

- ≈ Sensation identification

Ms. Morrish (MSc)

When I am either delivering a lecture or in consultation with educators, a scenario is often highlighted and explained in order for me to have a clearer understanding of behaviour(s) that adults feel is the concern. Such as when a child is:

- refusing to follow instructions

- being definat and removed themselves from the classroom

- rocking on their chair

- calling out and disrupting the lesion

- throwing objects across the classroom

Whatever the situation is, it is absolutely vital how the adult actually responds to this. The response to a behavioural situation will either decrease the behaviours that you do not want to see, or actually, believe it or not, increase the behaviours that you do want to see. Let us consider a child is calling out and is disrupting the flow of your lesson and interfering with the other children's attention.

I then ask, *"How did you respond?"* 99.9% of the time the response will be something along the lines of, *"Well, how I've responded is I've made sure that I've stated the classroom rules again."* Or, *"I followed the school policy and I told her that she will be inside for lunchtime reflection."* The explanation of their response was often presented in the form of a 'consequence. However, what has actually happened is that they have misunderstood HOW they have actually responded. Therefore, within *"Talking for a Purpose"* there are two types of responses: one is known as your initial response and the other is your secondary response.

Explanation of the term Initial Response

Your initial response is 99% physiological and is at the subconscious level. When Deshawn 'sucked his teeth', I can remember a surge of heat going through my body way before the words came falling out of my dysregulated mouth. Some teachers experience a hot left palm and others a tingling in their right thigh. I have had some teachers talk about a burning sensation in their chest and their neck and others a tingle on the tips of their fingers.

The significance of identifying your initial response is vital because if this is not managed, your secondary response will come out, without thought. Think of a cartoon character such as Bart Simpson. Bart often says things without thinking, which gets him into trouble. I remember an episode where Bart, blurted some hurtful words to his sister Lisa, in a big speech bubble. Then immediately he tried to swallow them back into his mouth as if the words were not said. How many times have you said words and immediately wanted to swallow them back? Words something along the line of, *"OK, now EVERYONE is in for breaktime,"* and, *"why do I have to ask you 100 times to listen?"* and, *"Would you do that at home?"* Does this sound familiar?

Ms. Morrish (MSc)

Explanation of Secondary Response

The second part of responses is what's called a secondary response. Quite simply, your secondary responses are your words; it is language. Your language to be more precise, it is the sentences that come out, just like Bart's, due to the fact that your initial response has not been recognised and managed BEFORE you speak.

So, imagine your initial response could be something like an increased heartbeat. You enter into a heightened state which leads to a decrease in your ability to stop and think before you speak.

In my experience, the most common secondary response is a redundant question. Redundant questions will be explained in chapter nine. For now, what often happens is the child responds to the question and you enter what is referred to as the cycle of defiance.

The Cycle of Defiance

What is the cycle of defiance?

I am sure there have been many times within your teaching career when you have felt that you are going 'back and forth' with a child. You believe that you have stated what you want regarding the child's behaviour, yet the compliance has not occurred. Perhaps you feel like you are not being heard? Or do you feel that you are constantly repeating yourself? Or that your class NEVER listens to you. If this sounds familiar to you, you have entered into the cycle of defiance.

See below for the illustration which will show the cycle in terms of redundant questions.

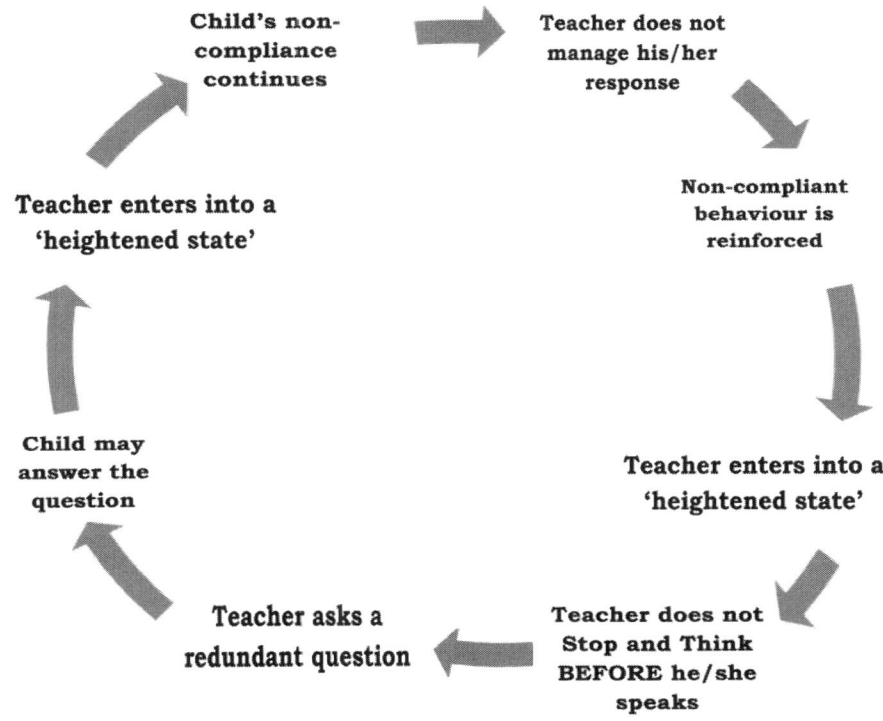

Ms. Morrish (MSc)

When examining the cycle in terms of redundant questions, the question then is; how do we break such a negative cycle?

The <u>only</u> thing that you have complete and total ownership over is <u>YOU</u>. This means your behaviour, not the child's. Now let us break down what I mean by behaviour. In its simplest form, the term behaviour can be viewed as the action or reaction to something under specified circumstances.

But what does this actually mean for you as a teacher? I personally feel that this means that you are accountable for all aspects of your behaviour. This includes your responses, language and actions.

Although there are additional variables to consider, such as the environment and, of course, who you are communicating with; however, I want to emphasise that although such variables may play a part, the most important elements are ownership over your complete behaviour. So, to answer the question above, <u>YOU</u> are the only part within the cycle that you have complete ownership over managing.

Practise out of Context

I would like to emphasise the preparation that is required of you as a teacher, to be able to manage your emotional state. If your initial response has *not* been identified and practised out of context, it is going to be much more challenging for you to be able to manage your behaviour and language when your 'behaviour button' has been pushed within your classroom.

The sensation will feel too big. It will feel much bigger and much more intense than it actually is, possibly resulting in you feeling even more anxious, worried or overwhelmed. Once you have identified your initial response out of context, I can virtually guarantee that it will be the same initial physiological response when you are in a classroom. By practicing, the sensations will no longer be new and will eventually become a positive association. This will result in you being much more confident and most importantly—prepared.

Example of Practising out of Context

Back in the UK, I was asked if I would implement *"Talking for a Purpose"* in a school just outside London. On my very first visit, a child sucked his teeth! I had not heard this for quite some time but oh wow, my initial response was the same. The heat through my body immediately followed by, *"Can you stop doing that please?"* To which he replied, *"Yes I can, but I won't."*

I knew that I had to develop a way in which I could manage this initial feeling in a proactive way. I knew that this behaviour was going to happen again in this school so I wanted to be prepared, but how? How can I prepare myself? I searched the internet, read books but I gained very little insight into effective strategies. One Sunday, I was having a rare Netflix afternoon and came across a program called Top Boy. Top Boy is a British television series, set in a fictional estate in Hackney, East London. Within ten minutes, the teeth sucking started, then again, and again.

What an ideal time to practise! So, each time the behaviour occurred, the main thing I did was slow my breathing down. Slowing my breath down helped me manage that hot sensation, and as a result I did not feel the heat so intensely. I did this throughout the whole first episode. If you have seen the show, you will know that I went through a lot of practise to manage my 'behaviour button'. Just by slowing down my breathing, I felt calmer and more in control of my thoughts. I also started to associate the button with calm.

Each time the behaviour occurred, I regulated myself into a calm resourceful state. Within this resourceful state, I had increased clarity and a reduction of words whirling around inside my head. I felt prepared.

Reflective Activity

You should, initially, identify what has created a physiological sensation somewhere in your body. Some examples are below:

- You are in the supermarket, and somebody takes the last trolley
- You are in a car park, and somebody takes that parking spot that you have been waiting patiently for and clearly had your indicator flashing.
- You are out in the park with your dog and somebody walks past and makes a comment around the fact that all dogs should be on leads.

- You have gone to Costa Coffee to finish an assignment and the WiFi suddenly stops working as your frustration increases. You snap at the person who just brought over your coffee, "*What's happened to the WiFi? I have a really important deadline to meet.*"

In all these situations, a physiological sensation occurs first, somewhere in your body.

Sensation Identification

Next, I want you to identify if there is some sensation somewhere in your body: heat, coldness, buzzing, tingling or flickering sensation. Does it have a colour? Is it so big that it covers your whole chest or smaller that it is just at the top of your head?

Think BEFORE You Speak

Now you have identified your initial response, before your secondary response comes out. You have probably heard the saying: Think before you speak.

This is important because while most of us can at times be somewhat careless with the words we choose, words are powerful. They can be helpful or hurtful, and can have a direct influence on the outcome of a situation, creating a positive or negative reaction within your classroom.

Ms. Morrish (MSc)

Words define our identity and reveal our attitudes and sensitivities, reflecting who we are. Our choice of word gives listeners an indication of our intelligence or ignorance. And when continually reinforced and turned into habitually negative thought patterns, they have the power to create a bad habit of dwelling on the negatives in life.

The problem is, once words exit our mouths, no number of apologies will make them magically go back in: blurting something out and then trying to retract it is like shutting the gate after the horse has bolted. On the other hand, thinking before we speak allows us time to consider the effect of the words we are choosing.

The issue that I have regarding the concept of thinking before speaking is that I believe that there is a significant element missing and that is 'stop'—adults have to 'stop' first. This is because, if an adult has not stopped what they are currently doing, the platform for the thinking decreases.

It is up to you to control your own tongue and take responsibility for what emerges from your mouth. Be prepared to <u>stop</u> and think before you speak, say what you mean, stand behind your statements and be responsible for them. One technique I use when working with educators to think before you speak is to find your internal 'stop' activator.

The voice in your head may be saying one thing, but your 'stop' activator will help you decide if it is something that should be said out loud.

Finding your internal 'stop' activator will support you to address situations that are present.

- Recognise your initial response—pay attention to physical reactions and sensations that are building in you, such as increased body heat or the feeling of a 'knot' in the stomach. Once you acknowledge your initial response, you can use it as a sign to activate your inner 'stop' activator.
- Mentally say 'stop' you could, for example additionally imagine you are at a traffic light which is displaying red. So, that you are matching a symbol with the word, which in turn will become a positive association.
- Regulated Breathing—this provides extra oxygen to your brain and assists with thought processes before speaking.
- Observe—listen to others. You may feel there is an obligation to say something all the time but there really is not. Instead, listen to your thoughts and observe them as they come and go.
- Mentally press 'play'—you are now in a more resourceful state to 'respond and not react'.

It may seem that doing the above requires a lot of time and effort, and if you have trained your mind to always immediately react, it will seem like that at first. But the inner 'stop' activator is a simple reminder to yourself that you are allowed to wait and take the time to respond appropriately. Even just a few extra seconds of thinking time can make a huge difference, so simply allowing yourself to stop, allows you to make a better choice as to how to proceed.

Ms. Morrish (MSc)

|CHAPTER EIGHT|

The Managing State Model (MSM) - Managing Your 'Heightened State'

'If I am truly honest, initially I wasn't convinced. I have been teaching as a senior leader for eight years. I am in a 'challenging school' and I have to say, what Ms. Morrish taught us has changed our whole school approach. The Managing State Model is so effective, who else teaches that practicality?'

Mr Simson,

SENCO and lead for behaviour

By the end of this chapter, you will have a clear understand of the following:

- ≈ What is meant by the term Heightened State?
- ≈ The relevance within education.
- ≈ The physiological impact upon teacher's behaviour.
- ≈ How to manage your Heightened State.
- ≈ The three components of the Managing State Model (MSM).
- ≈ The impact of your rate of speech and behavioural compliance.

Ms. Morrish (MSc)

You hear the first bell ring for the end of lunchtime play. You know you have approximately six minutes to be in your classroom, at the door which leads to the playground. You are waiting for the Mid-Day Assistant to line the children up so they can enter the learning environment.

As soon as the door opens you hear loudly, *"No, wait, wait I said"* from the MDA. Just as Connor storms into the classroom and shouts, *"Ms Jones, Jacob fucking hit me."* You look immediately to the MDA, who is still trying to speak yet all you now hear is a loud, *"It was Jacob, he fucking hit me when we were playing football."* You bring the rest of the class inside and attempt to speak to Connor who then states, *"This school is a shit-show!"* and goes under the table.

Before I continue, I would like you to note that within this example, I am completely aware that there are multiple factors that may have attributed to Connor's behaviour:

1. His Nan *may* have recently passed away.
2. He *may* not have taken his ADHD medication that morning.
3. He *may* have been told before entering the playground 'that if his behaviour continued, he would not be able to play in the school's football match tomorrow.'
4. The MDA *may* have stated that as he was not listening, his teacher was going to move his name down to red on the classroom chart.
5. He *may* not have had breakfast this morning because it was his weekend at Dads and his new girlfriends' house. The list goes on.

"Talking for a Purpose"

In general terms, a school will have a Behaviour Policy in place whereby the adult would deliver an appropriate consequence for Connor's behaviour. Adults should then address the possible triggers for the behaviour so that it occurs less frequently, or ideally, not at all. Some educators will deliver what they view as an appropriate consequence which is influenced by the possible trigger.

Others will deliver a consistent consequence, then examine the triggers so that the environment, the child and the adult's behaviour in order to put appropriate behaviour interventions in place. I understand the importance of a 'safe space' for children so that they can reset and self-regulate. I understand the core concepts; in fact, I play a significant part, as a consultant to support schools to examine triggers and develop consistent behaviour interventions for children. Yet, what I want to address here is what happens at that time for the adult.

How do we know that the adult who is attempting to talk to, or support Connor in that moment is not in fact; 're-triggering' him? I have spent my whole career working with such a dynamic range of educators. From the trainee teachers and NQTs, to the executive head teachers, the school administration personnel and senior teachers. All of which had different years of experience; and all with varying experience. Yet, no matter who it is, no matter how experienced, the adult will often go into what I term a 'heightened state'.

Ms. Morrish (MSc)

The Relevance within Education

So, the question arises how are, you going to manage your emotional internal state before speaking within a classroom to ensure that your secondary response is appropriate and is what you want to say. When people talk about managing a heightened state, people often ask, how is this relevant within the classroom and how is this relevant within education? In my opinion, I feel that this is possibly one of the most relevant aspects with regards to classroom management. Let us take a moment to consider the concept. When I am talking about an emotional internal state, I am thinking around those negative internal feelings such as feeling worried, anxious, concerned, or devalued. These feelings then impact your behaviour, your language, your thought process and your perceived behavioural outcomes.

What is a 'Heightened State'?

To help describe the term heightened state, let us consider some of the following.

Have you ever been in a situation where you had to manage a child who has displayed one or more of the following:

1. Deliberately damaged school property
2. Hurt an adult or peer deliberately
3. Set off the school fire alarm
4. Racial comments towards an adult or peer

> High Level Behaviours

1. Said NO straight to your face
2. Ripped up their work
3. Refused to follow adult's instructions

> Moderate Level Behaviours

1. Calling out
2. Rocking on a chair
3. Walking around the classroom

> Lower Level Behaviours

The Biological Impact on Teacher's Behaviour

The reaction begins in your amygdala, the part of your brain responsible for perceived fear. The amygdala responds by sending signals to the hypothalamus, which stimulates the autonomic nervous system (ANS). The ANS consists of the sympathetic and parasympathetic nervous systems. The sympathetic nervous system drives the fight-or-flight response, while the parasympathetic nervous system drives freezing.

Therefore, in general what happens, is your ANS is stimulated and your nervous system responds by releasing a flood of stress hormones, including adrenaline and cortisol, which rouse the body for emergency action. Cortisol is produced by our adrenal glands to help us regulate blood pressure, cardiovascular function and the way the body uses proteins, carbohydrates and fat. You may have heard of the 'fight or flight' syndrome.

The reason I mention this is because cortisol secretion increases in response to physical and psychological stress, which is why it is often referred to as the 'stress hormone'. Your heart may pound slightly faster, muscles may tighten, blood pressure may rise and you may experience an increase in shallow breathing. How many times can you relate to this while in your school?

Now there are some behaviours particularly those classified as higher-level concerns that you as a teacher need to respond to quickly and effectively; such as when a child brings a knife into school. You will require adrenaline in order to increase your alertness and act fast. However, with regard to those behaviours which do not require such a rapid response, the adult will still experience some increase physiologically. It could be an increased heart beat and slightly sweaty palms when a child refuses to complete his/her work.

One aspect that often puts adults into a heightened state is when they may feel anxious or frustrated. For example, if a child continues to interrupt your lesson by getting up and wondering around the classroom, frustration may set in. Or you may start to feel anxious when the child who you have instructed to turn off the computer actually doesn't follow instructions just as the head teacher walks by.

However, whatever the physiological reaction is, the one commonality that I see time and time again, is this—when adults are in a heightened state, they talk! Then talk some more! The words just seem to start flooding out without much thought. I hear adults stating non-relatable consequences, I hear negotiations with the child, I even hear bribery, and of course the most frequent is asking a redundant question.

How to manage your Heightened State

Professionals who are trained and practised in Neuro Linguistic Programming, better known as NLP, believe that there is no such thing as an un-resourceful person, just an un-resourceful state.

Being able to manage your state so that you are able to remain calm and resourceful even in the most challenging of situations is clearly something that is immensely significant within educational settings.

All states are caused by the interaction between your thinking patterns, your physiology and your neurochemicals. Changing any of these can influence <u>your</u> internal state.

Managing State Model (MSM)

I developed a model utilising some simple elements that educators can implement to manage their internal emotional state, when they have become heightened. There are four components within the model which will now be explained:

Component 1: Regulated Breathing

So, yes, we need to breathe to be alive. However, in order to change your emotional, internal state; so as to be in a more resourceful state, you need to control your breathing. Sounds simple, and you have possibly heard the saying, hold your breath and count to ten. Yet when in a heightened state, your breathing will quicken and the more frustrated you become.

Therefore, one thing to do is what is called controlled breathing or regulated breathing. Regulated breathing changes your neurological state. It immediately slows everything down. So, the regulated count of breathing I suggest to teachers is often breathing in for a count of six, hold for four and out for six. Regulated breathing increases the supply of oxygen to your brain and stimulates the parasympathetic nervous system, which promotes a state of calmness.

Now, please note that I am not by any means suggesting that you lay on the floor, with your hands on your tummy doing controlled breathing. However, remember the significance of practising out of context as highlighted throughout this book. People will not even know that you are doing it because taking in a breath and letting it go is invisible.

You can train yourself. You do so by taking the time to practise, controlling your breathing rate out of the classroom. You will be able to get into a resourceful state much quicker when required in the classroom. The regulated breathing helps you to be in a much more resourceful state, so that you are clear about your behavioural instructions and state the consequences of what you actually mean to say.

Time

You may be reading this thinking, *"I don't have time to do breathing exercises!"* Well, I am here to tell you that you do. You have so much more time than you perceive you have. Connor is under the table and is safe. Not damaging school property or swearing, just under the table. So, he is just refusing to come out for various reasons.

The other children have gone to assembly or gone out to play, or are in the classroom doing what they are supposed to be doing. And Connor is under the table and he is just refusing to come out. So you have TIME to manage your heightened state and therefore know what you are going to say and how you are going to say it, when YOU are ready.

Component 2: Posture

One of the other aspects of supporting you to manage your emotional internal state before you speak is your posture. When it comes to posture, I am not talking about standing unnaturally straight as a rod, looking all menacing and intimidating, because that is actually the last thing that you really want to be portraying as an educator. However, your posture is massively significant with regards to managing your internal state.

Think about those people who are, for whatever reason, not positive, seeing the glass half empty most of the time. I often refer to these people as mood hoovers; they hoover up your mood. So, you are in a group and everyone is positive and you are in the staff room. Then your co-worker starts to say comments such as: *"They don't ever listen"* or *"Why am I always the one on playground duty?"* (moan, moan and moan) hovering up everyone's positive mood. Or it could be somebody who is not even in your school. May be a friend or family member, cousin, your aunt, your brother, your sister that for whatever reason, just do not have a positive outlook on life.

Reflective Activity

I want you to take 30 seconds to picture a person that you have interacted with, or seen them interacting with somebody else. Imagine this person in front of you. Note their body stance, their posture; what do they look like? I can pretty much guarantee that they are slightly hunched over looking down on the floor and the frequency of their words is high.

Your posture has an impact on your brain, and on your thoughts. Psychologists have taken this observation as a basis for their research about the connection between mind and body. The scientific term used to best describe this characteristic is called Embodiment. Remember your thoughts become your words; to become your actions. So, just recognise how you are standing or sitting.

- ≈ Are you slouching over?
- ≈ Do you slouch?
- ≈ Do you have your hands on your hips?

- ≈ Do you have a hip movement?
- ≈ Is that when you are relaxed?
- ≈ Is that when you are confident?
- ≈ Is that when you are conveying a really positive message?
- ≈ Or is it the opposite?

The single thing that you can do is simply push your shoulders back, and sit up straighter. Standing straight; impacts your physiological makeup within your physiological state which then has a positive impact on your thoughts and behaviour. Bear in mind, I am not talking about a power pose where you stand in front of your class like Superman, Wonder Woman, or even Usain Bolt. However, one thing I really want you to understand is that when you look unsure, you will sound unsure.

Change your posture, stand tall, high and successful, not only will you look confident but you'll feel more confident. Therefore, you will sound more confident when delivering a behaviour instruction. Consider changing your facial expression too, even the smallest amends will help you manage your state. Then managing your state will help you to also manage your words, and remember, your words have the impact upon not just children, but on everyone who hears them.

Component 3: Movement

Change your body radically—move, do anything that pushes different chemicals around your nervous system such as simply moving away from the table where Connor is under. Or just simply walk across the classroom. Your mind and body are intimately connected. And while your brain is the master control system for your body's movement, the way you move can also affect the way you think and feel and therefore respond. While it may appear obvious that your feelings can influence your movement, it is not as obvious that your movement can impact your feelings too. For example, when you feel tired and sad, you may move more slowly. When you feel anxious, you may appear to be more rushed and in a hurry. However, let us consider that the connection between your brain and your body is bi-directional which means movement can change your thought processes too.

Component 4: Eye Gaze

When I am working with educators who are not in a resourceful state, their eye movement is often looking down. Now depending on whether the person is right or left-handed, their eye gaze which is down and to the left or right; is classified by the NLP practitioners as the individual retrieving information kinaesthetically.

Or put simply, accessing feelings. Now, if the feelings are frustration or anxiousness, looking down will only be reinforcing those negative feelings which then reinforces the negative thoughts such as: *"Why do they listen to the teacher and not me?"*, or "T*heir teacher from last year said she had no problems regarding behaviour."*

Maybe even: *"I really don't think I am good enough to pass my NQT year."* These thoughts will then impact your behaviour. The key point here is, look up when giving a behavioural instruction. More importantly, keep looking up if the behaviour has not been carried out.

The Impact of Your Rate of Speech

After many years developing the Managing State Model, I noticed a very important aspect regarding internal states. What I consistently observed is that once a person enters a heightened state it very difficult for them to slow their words down, primarily due to the adrenaline and noradrenaline running through their body.

Consequently, the rate of speech actually increases, making it hard for the child to process instructions and enabling the adult to remain in a heightened state. So, I decided to flip this concept. What if the rate of speech was slowed down, in turn reducing the amount of adrenaline within the body, which in turn enables adults to remain in a resourceful state and manage the behaviour concerned?

What I discovered is that it is extremely difficult for a person to remain in a heightened state once they have slowed their rate of speech down. It is a powerful technique, slow your rate of speech and become within a resourceful state. Then you know what you are going to say with a measured behavioural outcome.

Ms. Morrish (MSc)

Reflective Activity

Task 1: Think about a time when you were experiencing negative emotions such as attending a funeral of a relative. People around you were sad and expressive.

How was their rate of speech; fast or slow?

_____

Task 2: Think about a time where you attended a wedding. The people around you were happy.

How was their rate of speech? Fast or slow?

_____

Task 3: The next time you are in a situation where non-compliance is occurring, I want you to monitor your rate of speech.

If you think you are talking slowly, I want you to go even slower.

Then take note of the positive impact upon behaviour compliance.

What was the difference that you noticed?

_____

_____

"Talking for a Purpose"

|CHAPTER NINE|

Redundant Questions

"When Ms. Morrish teaches you about Redundant Questions you think to yourself, "That is obvious, I never do that." Then you hear yourself, and those around you using them regularly! The awareness of your own language, eliminates them and increases the children's compliance."

Mrs Burrell, Head Teacher

By the end of this chapter, you will have a clear understanding of the following:

- ≈ A definition of the term Redundant Question and the criteria that makes the Question Redundant.
- ≈ The difference between a Redundant Question and a Rhetorical Question.
- ≈ The common categories of Redundant Questions that are consistently asked within classrooms.
- ≈ The reasons why Redundant Questions are asked.
- ≈ The self-evaluating question that you internally ask yourself, to ensure the question is not redundant.
- ≈ The significance of the word 'sometimes' when asking a possible Redundant Question.

Ms. Morrish (MSc)

Redundant questions are everywhere. I constantly hear them in schools, supermarkets, playgrounds. In fact, in any environment where adults and children interact, I will hear redundant questions. So, what do I mean by the term redundant questions?

A definition of the term Redundant Question and the criteria that makes the question redundant

A redundant question is a question that does not need to be asked. The question is not related to what you as the teacher actually want to happen. Unfortunately, the children's answers are not what you want to hear. Children's responses to redundant questions often annoy, or even infuriate the questioner, as the answers are usually extremely relevant and precise to the question that has been asked.

The difference between a Redundant Question and a Rhetorical Question

Many teachers can initially get a little confused about what a redundant question is. Many people have asked: *"Well, isn't a redundant question, the same as a rhetorical question?"* The answer is no, they are not the same thing.

Let us take a moment to clarify the difference. A **rhetorical** question is one for which the questioner does not expect a direct answer; in many cases it may be intended to start a discourse, or as a means of putting across the speaker's or author's opinion on a topic. (Gideon O. Burton, 2007)

A rhetorical question is also often said in humour. When the person is asking the question, says it in a humorous way, and isn't really expecting an answer. Some really basic examples are: *"Is the Pope Catholic?"* or, *"Do bears live in the woods"*. Another example is, if you have ever been late, someone might ask: *"What time do you call this?"* This person does not want an actual answer to the question.

With a rhetorical question there is a purpose to the question and the person has thought it through before speaking and it is a question asked to make a point, rather than get an answer. A redundant question, on the other hand, is a question that a teacher asks because they have not self-regulated. The question has not been thought through. Let us look at a simple example of a four-year-old child who is not following the instructions the first time.

The teacher responds with the question, *"Why don't you follow instructions the first time?"* Is this *really* what the teacher *wanted* to ask? The teacher failed to stop and think before speaking. Therefore, the question asked is not actually what the teacher wanted to say and is therefore redundant in the situation. With redundant questions, children of all ages are absolute experts at answering them.

So even for your least challenging children, these children will often answer the question that has been asked. Of course, what then happens is, that child is seen as being possibly defiant, rude and possibly a little bit cheeky. However, how many times have you heard a redundant question to which a child answers, leading to the teacher giving a negative consequence to the child? So, my question in this whole scenario is, who should be held accountable? My answer is <u>you</u>.

The reasons why Redundant Questions are asked Heightened State

Here is the biggest difference between a rhetorical question and redundant question. A rhetorical question is asked with a purpose and has been thought through by the questioner before the question has been asked. A redundant question is asked when a teacher is in a heightened state.

This heightened state may be due to the teacher feeling frustrated at the perception of not being heard. Or it could be negative energy or anxiety as they are being observed by the head teacher. It may even be due to tiredness as your three-year-old daughter has a cough that has limited both hers and your own sleep. Whatever the reason, the words start to come out in the form of a question, a question that you <u>do not</u> want an answer to.

The issue with redundant questions is that they are everywhere. Reflect honestly; have you ever asked a redundant question? Do you often hear your colleagues asking them? Can you remember your own teachers asking you a redundant question when you were at school?

When I deliver workshops and lectures, I ask the audience, *"Who amongst you have asked a redundant question previously?"* and every time, no matter the audience 95% of people raise their hands. So, let us consider some of the possibilities as to why they are so common an occurrence. Another possible explanation is that you were likely that were asked redundant question by your parents.

Can you think of some examples?

Additionally, I remember being at school, particularly my secondary school, and my teachers would ask me multiple redundant questions, to which I took complete pleasure in answering. Which is possibly why I had my own designated seat; in detention.

The Common Categories of Redundant Questions Consistently asked within Classrooms

There are common categories or starting words that are linked to redundant questions. There are some categories that are said more frequently than others. Before I give examples, please take a moment and complete the reflective activity outlined below.

Reflective Activity

Take a moment and think about the times when you have asked a question that you did not actually want to ask.

Ms. Morrish (MSc)

Then write down six questions on a separate page which upon reflection, were redundant. Include all your words that came tumbling out.

Now highlight the first word in each of your questions. Is there some commonality in the first word or are they all different?

This is what I mean by the term common category.

It basically means the word that starts the question. There are three common categories that are said most frequently within classrooms.

Can you think of them?

"Talking for a Purpose"

The three most common Redundant Questions are:

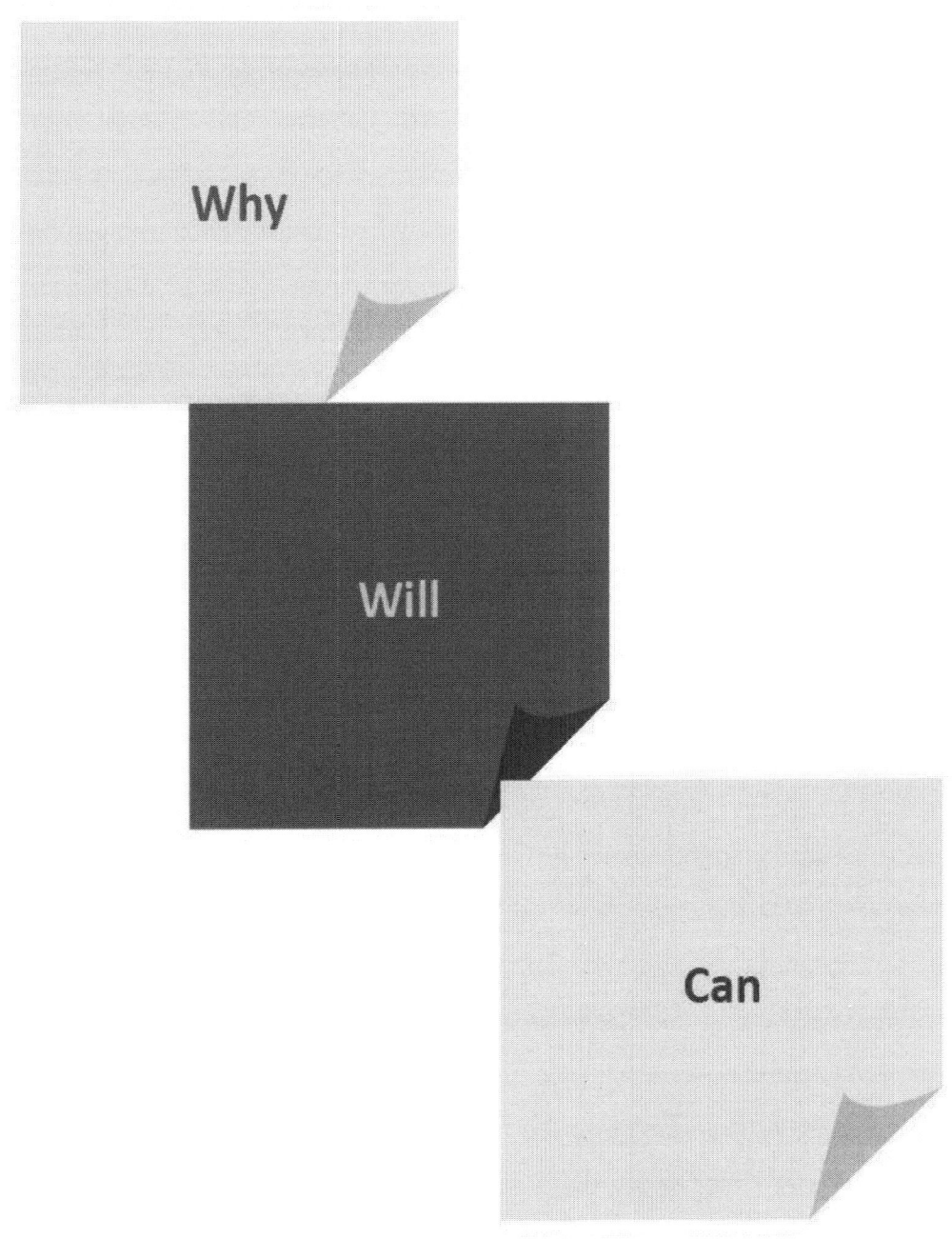

Ms. Morrish (MSc)

The Whys

- Why do I have to ask you a hundred times?
- Why don't you ever listen?
- Why are you running?
- Why are you talking?
- Why aren't you doing your work?
- Why do I bother even trying to help you?

The Wills

- Will you ever grow up?
- Will you ever be able to walk without me having to tell you?
- Will you ever understand what a good choice is?
- Will you sit still for once?
- Will you listen today?
- Will you stop acting like a fool?

The Cans

- Can you stop talking?
- Can you stop calling out?
- Can you listen for once?
- Can you even be bothered?
- Can you behave yourself?
- Can you behave more like your sister?

"Talking for a Purpose"

Here are some real-life examples!

Adult Redundant Question	Childs Response
Why do I have to ask you a hundred times?	Because you're a rubbish teacher No, this is only number 99 Because it's fun
Why are you running?	I am late for class It is quicker if you run I am a fast runner, watch
Will you ever grow up?	I hope so I don't want to be this size forever I am only 6
Can you listen for once?	What did you say? Something about listening OK but only once

Ms. Morrish (MSc)

These are real-life classroom examples that I have collated over the years and I can think of many more. Some you may even consider to be quite amusing, others possibly a rude response which may lead to a negative consequence. Yet again, who is accountable for asking the question?

Let us now examine the self-evaluating question that you internally ask yourself, to ensure the question is not redundant.

The Self-Evaluating Question

The self-evaluating question that you internally ask yourself, to ensure the question is not redundant. Remember the phrase 'stop and think before you speak'? There is a self-evaluating question during the 'think' part. It is part of an internal dialogue to ensure that the question you are about to ask isn't redundant.

It is really straightforward. It is simply, do I want an answer to the question? If you want an answer to the question, ask it, and if not change it. However, the internal dialogue, the internal self-evaluating question, in my experience, is often only asked when the adult is in a calm, relaxed state.

So, the stopping activator that we have spoken about earlier is vital. But the thinking part for you is before you ask a question make sure that your question is not redundant. And to reiterate, ask the internal question, do I want an answer? Try it. You will be surprised.

The Significance regarding the Word 'Sometimes' when asking a Possible Redundant Question

Consider the importance of the self-evaluation question if you are questioning the validity of the redundant question. Because sometimes the redundant question is appropriate. When thinking about redundant questions, first accept that not all why questions, will questions, can questions, what questions, and how questions are redundant.

Because within context; some of those questions are relevant. I ask many why questions to both children and adults that I work with. So, what makes these categories that have been previously identified now as relevant and appropriate questions?

What makes a why question, for example, not redundant?

The difference is that a teacher has stopped to think BEFORE he or she has spoken. So, they are self-regulated or have self-managed themselves. The teacher has identified their initial response, managed the response BEFORE the secondary response comes tumbling out of their mouth in the form of a redundant question. They have accessed the self-evaluating question of; do I want an answer? to ensure that the question is not redundant.

That is where the word 'sometimes' becomes a definite. You are going to ask the question with a purpose. The question that you are about to ask, has a definite purpose, because you genuinely want an answer.

Ms. Morrish (MSc)

Redundant Statement

'I still can't believe that just a simple change in my language has such a huge positive affect within my classroom. Change your language, you won't regret it!'

James Wright, Year Three Teacher

It is considered standard within most, if not all books on classroom management, to highlight the importance of asking for what you want, not what you don't want. So why is it that I hear high frequencies of redundant statements on a daily basis when consulting in schools?

By the end of this section, you will have a clear understanding of the following:

- ≈ The term Redundant Statement
- ≈ The reason why this is classed as redundant

In the previous chapter, I explained and have suggested numerous examples of redundant questions. However, in *"Talking for a Purpose"*, there is only <u>one</u> redundant statement. The reason that the statement becomes redundant is due to the fact that there is a school of thought suggesting that the brain doesn't always filter a negative.

"Talking for a Purpose"

What this means is that when the brain hears this word, it does not have the ability to think, hold on to the image and realise it actually means something else.

Can you think of the redundant statement?

If so, give an example.

_____

_____

Reflective Activity 1

1. Take a few minutes to write down all the words that could possibly begin the redundant statement.

_____

_____

Ms. Morrish (MSc)

> 2. Then close your eyes and ask another adult to say, "*Open your eyes, don't think of a pink elephant?*"
>
>   a. Did you see a pink elephant?

The problem with this word is that your subconscious mind does not understand the word; don't. I often give a little exercise by asking everyone to close their eyes, then I have them open their eyes and then I tell them, *"Don't think of a pink elephant."*

Approximately 80% of the audience will then tell me that is exactly what they thought of, but not everybody. It is also my understanding that this has nothing to do with intellect, whether you see the pink elephant or not. It is just how your brain filters the incoming message.

However, let us now apply the same 80% to the children in your classroom. How many children in your classroom would not be able to filter the don't?

That is right; the majority will continue to display the behaviours that you have asked them not to do. Therefore, you are actually asking for what you don't want.

"Talking for a Purpose"

Reflective Activity 2

Write a list of phrases starting with don't that you have either said yourself or heard your colleagues stating. I have added two examples for you.

Can you give another four examples and let us consider what the children may possibly be hearing?

___

___

	Give a *don't* example	**What is the child/children actually hearing?**
1	Don't call out	Call out
2	Don't run	Run

Ms. Morrish (MSc)

Reflective Activity 3

If you have another adult in your classroom, such as a Teaching Assistant, ask them to note when you say any phrases starting with don't. You will be surprised.

Practising out of Context

You can practise when you are out of context such as when you are in a supermarket, in the gym, on the bus, or train. Even when you are just out with your friends and family, listen out for anyone starting a phrase with don't and you will be surprised how often this word is used. Then just observe what happens.

"Don't think of a pink elephant. This really has stuck with me and every single day I make a conscious decision about the language that I use with my class and the way I deliver instructions."

Alexandra Hall, Year One Teacher

"Talking for a Purpose"

|CHAPTER TEN|

Exact Moment Behaviour (EMB)

'The BEST part of my behaviour management training as a trainee teacher was learning about and then implementing Exact Moment Behaviours straight away in my placement. I now pass on the magic to my NQT's each and every year.'

Anna Dayson, Assistant Head Teacher

By the end of this chapter, you will have a clear understanding of the following:

- ≈ The term Perceived Behaviour Outcome (PBO).
- ≈ The term Exact Moment Behaviour (EMB).
- ≈ Classroom examples which are not exact moment behaviour, yet frequently stated in classrooms.
- ≈ Teacher Identified Concerns (TIC).
- ≈ The EMB self-evaluating question.
- ≈ How to replace Redundant Questions with an Exact Moment Behaviour.
- ≈ The significance of stopping the current behaviour first.
- ≈ Guidelines to correctly implement stopping the current behaviour first.
- ≈ The difference between stop and don't.

≈ A note regarding please and thank you in order to increase positive behaviours.

As previously stated in the previous chapter, that teachers should always ask for what you want, not what you don't want. In its simplicity this sounds effective. However, during my twenty years consulting within a variety of educational establishments, I still constantly hear educators not stating clearly the behaviour they actually want to see or hear in that <u>exact moment</u>.

Perceived Behaviour Outcome

When I coach teachers, they often state that they feel under pressure due to the volume of work required of them to teach each and every lesson. This, coupled with the general school timetable can create difficulties in stating the behaviour you actually want in that moment, as it is more natural to jump ahead to your perceived behavioural outcome.

An example of a Perceived Behaviour Outcome (PBO)

Let us take a simple example of your class having to be on time for an assembly to start. Your thoughts tend to focus on what I term a perceived behavioural outcome. In this example, your PBO may be your whole class lined up and ready to leave the classroom, as it is now time for the whole school assembly.

"Talking for a Purpose"

You clearly stated your instruction to the whole class, once the children are quiet and sitting in their chairs facing you. *"I would like everyone to stand up and walk quietly to line up please."* However, some children that are, actually not ready to line up due to the fact that they are still fiddling with their pencil, rocking on their chair and still talking to their friends.

Yet your thought process regarding perceived behaviour outcome, is everyone lining up quietly. In fact, what is required in such situations is that you have to be present and 'in the moment'. However, you notice a child still tapping his/her pen on the white board or swinging on his/her chair. In this scenario, what would your reaction be?

Here are some examples that I hear in classrooms to the scenario described above:

- *"Why have you not lined up with everyone else?"*
- *"I have asked everyone to line up and that includes you."*
- *"Can you line up, please?"*
- *"Quickly, you are making us late for assembly."*
- *"Ok, now go to the back of the line."*

Do any of these questions sound familiar to you?

Ms. Morrish (MSc)

Are they possibly redundant questions?

What is an Exact Moment Behaviour?

The term Exact Moment Behaviour (EMB) is exactly as described in the title. It is the **ONLY** behaviour that you ask for in **THAT EXACT MOMENT**. Your Exact Moment Behaviour is the behaviour that you want to see or hear **in that moment.**

Examples of Frequently Stated Non-Exact Moment Behaviours in Classrooms

Examples that are not EMBs include teachers saying, *"Stop calling out."* and, *"You are walking around the classroom."* or, *"You are making too much noise"* as well as, *"You are talking over me."* and *"You are still rocking on your chair."* or, *"You are distracting your peers from learning."* The list is endless. Just take a moment and re-read the examples and I am sure you can think of several of your own that you have either said yourself or heard your colleagues saying.

Do these statements actually support children to modify their behaviour? In my experience, the answer is no. The behaviour that the teacher doesn't want is actually often repeated. By taking careful note of the words used in each example, has the teacher actually stated what he or she wants instead? The answer is no.

Question: Is this an exact moment behaviour? Does this state what you actually want?

Teacher Identified Concern (TIC)

Classroom Example

Let us take an example of a child calling out while the teacher is delivering input for English in a Year Three classroom. During the input, Billy calls out, *"I know the answer to this Mrs Brown, my dad told me.'* The teacher responds with, *"Billy, remember the rules, you need to raise your hand when you know the answer."*

Yet Billy does know the answer and he does raise his hand yet still calls out. Billy is now seen as not following instructions and not following the classroom expectations.

Ms. Morrish (MSc)

The teacher says again, *"Billy, remember the rules, you need to raise your hand when you know the answer."* Billy raises his hand as instructed and says *"But Mrs Brown I do know the answer, my dad told me over the weekend. It is James and the Giant Peach."*

"Billy as you are not following classroom expectations even after two reminders, please go and move your peg down the orange." Billy stands up as instructed and completes the walk of shame across the classroom to find his name on the classroom chart.

He moves his peg down to the orange square, while his peers watch. He mutters to himself *"But I do know the answer."* Deflated, he re-joins his classmates only to call out again later in the same session. Yes, he finished the session on 'red' and was kept in during break time.

However, Billy <u>has</u> followed the teacher's instructions. The teacher clearly stated, *"You need to raise your hand when you know the answer."*

The issue here is that the teacher has not been specific enough with her exact moment behaviour. The teacher has not stopped to think what she actually wants instead of Billy calling out. She is feeling somewhat annoyed that she is being interrupted and that he is not following classroom expectations.

When I am in consultation with school staff and a situation such as this has occurred, the teacher will often state their perceived behaviour outcome. When I ask, *"What do you want instead?"* the answer is always for him to do his work or for her to listen and follow instructions the first time.

However, the central concern is not either of these, it is, in fact, the key element that this teacher and hundreds of teachers miss. The behaviour that is causing the primary concern is not lack of work or not following instructions. The primary concern is <u>noise</u>. Billy's calling out is in fact <u>sound</u>.

There are two key words that are missing from the teacher's instructions. Can you think of them?

To make the concept of exact moment behaviour easier to understand, I teach it in regards to what you want instead <u>in that moment</u>. One of the best ways to think about this is to think about your EMB behaviour as the opposite to what you are experiencing. To support your thinking, we will come back to this example after the next activity.

Replacing Redundant Questions with an Exact Moment Behaviour

Let us look at some common redundant questions

Possible redundant question	Presenting behaviour (What is the behaviour that you need to replace?)	Your EMB (What do you want instead?)

Ms. Morrish (MSc)

'Will you stop calling out?'		
'Why are you running?'		
'Can you stop pushing?'		
'Can you stop tapping that pencil?'		
'Why are you out of your seat again?'		

Reflective Activity

Think about a time when you have been teaching and you have stated what you thought was a positive and clear behavioural instruction, yet you did not get your desired behaviour from the child. Write down some sentences that you have stated within your classroom. What could you now change in order for you to see and or hear the behaviour that <u>you</u> want?

EMB Self Evaluating Question

Before stating your exact moment behaviour, there is a self-evaluating question that you should internally ask yourself. Most people get confused with the self-evaluating question of a redundant question of *'do I want an answer?'*

The self-evaluating question is still your internal dialogue. This internal dialogue is to ensure that what you are about to say is specifically the behaviour that you want to see and/or hear in that exact moment.

It is simply…………

The word ***now*** should be starred, highlighted with arrows on it. The most important part of your self-evaluating question that you ask yourself <u>before</u> you state an exact moment behaviour is, what do I want him or her to do right <u>now</u>? Then think, in this exact moment.

Remember it is not your perceived behavioural outcome. It is in the moment. If a child is calling out, think of a replacement that **you** want. Remember calling out is sound so it is the sound/noise that requires the EMB. If a child is rocking on a chair, it is the <u>chair</u> that requires the EMB. If a child is tapping a pencil, it is the <u>pencil</u> that requires the EMB.

Teachers often struggle to be in the moment. As stated previously, there is so much pressure upon teaching staff throughout each school day. It is absolutely imperative that adults just take a second to stop and think before they speak. Similarly, as with redundant questions, if you do not take this time before you speak, the wrong words are going to come out. Then, you are going to find that you need to backtrack in order to state the behaviour that you actually want to happen in that moment.

The ability to correctly deliver an exact moment behaviour lies primarily in your ability to self-regulate, to take that second to just internally ask yourself that simple self-evaluating question, what do I want him, her or them to do now? From this, you will find that your behavioural instructions will become a series of exact moment behaviours, leading to behaviour compliance.

Stopping the Current Behaviour First

A common word that I hear in classrooms is the word stop. Stop is a powerful word, because it is an action; just as long as you are actually stating the behaviour that you want to stop. Take for example something as non-descript and generic as *'stop doing that'*.

This is very obviously not a clear instruction at all. 'Stop doing that' is not stating anything constructive. What happens is, the child receiving this information has to:

1. Understand the words
2. Understand what you are asking
3. Filter out irrelevant information
4. Process that information
5. Make a decision about what they are going to do.

Remember throughout *"Talking for a Purpose"* the focus is always on clarity and precision with your words, and this means taking ownership of your language.

Remember, the person who is communicating is the one who is accountable, and that is you. It is certainly not clear enough for children who struggle with attention, who can be defiant and oppositional because it is just not giving them enough information to make a positive behavioural decision.

However, possibly a more frequent adult instruction consists of the word <u>stop</u> and the behaviour that they no longer want to see. For example:

- *"Stop calling out"*
- *"Stop running"*
- *"Stop tapping"*
- *"Stop interrupting me"*
- *"Stop being silly"*

Ms. Morrish (MSc)

The Guidelines to Correctly Implement Stopping the Current Behaviour First

There are two aspects within these guidelines:

Aspect one: Clearly and precisely, state the behaviour that you want to stop.

- After just reading aspect one, you may be thinking 'how does that make sense'?
- Are you just then just telling the child what you don't want them to do?
- This sounds contradictory to the previous chapters, right?

Rationale: You are going to be really explicit with the behaviour that you want to stop, for both you as the communicator, and the child receiving the information, in order to get the bi-directional communication crystal clear. Remember, you are going to keep your words short, clear and precise. This immediately reduces the opportunity for misunderstanding the presenting behaviour for both yourself and the child.

Presenting Behaviour – pen/pencil tapping

Adults states - **"*STOP*"** + "*tapping your pencil/pen*"

What did you say next? Anything at all?

Aspect Two: Straight away, state your EMB.

STOP + Presenting Behaviour + Exact Behaviour

"tapping your pencil/pen"+"put your pencil/pen on the table"

Within this simple example, ask yourself, *"Could I be even clearer?"* For example, *"Put your pen on your white board."* Would you then state another EMB? Remember, as previously stated, behaviour compliance can often be viewed as a series or a sequences of exact moment behaviours.

Please note that you can add your EMB to support your existing classroom expectations. For example, *"Raise your hand and wait in silence, until I call your name."* The most important element is that you have to state your EMB.

The difference between Stop and Don't

I am often asked what is the difference between stop and don't. The simple difference is this, stop is an action, while don't is redundant as the brain fails to filter it as a negative.

Ms. Morrish (MSc)

A note about Please and Thank You

I am a stickler for manners, from children and particularly from adults. Before each and every presentation that I deliver, I will on purpose wait at optimal times to give out my handouts sporadically. This is strategic as I want to hear how the participants respond. Will you be surprised to know that consistently under 50% of adults say *thank you*? One of the behavioural concerns that is raised continually within schools is children's lack of respect and lack of manners.

Yet my question is, are ALL adults CONSISTENTLY modelling the behaviours that they CONSISTENTLY want to see and hear from children. Within the school environment, every single adult is accountable for his or her behaviour and language including please and thank you, for example.

There may be many children within your class and school where their home life does not lend itself to positive models of behaviour or language. Therefore, the next modelling environment is school.

Many people ask me about saying please or thank you when delivering a behaviour command. My first response is to always check your school's policy on behaviour. Some schools have very clear guidelines in terms of when you say please, for example at the beginning of the behaviour instruction.

The other aspect that is asked is saying thank you. There is an old approach that many schools appear to still adopt and that is to say thank you at the end of every behaviour instruction. The thinking around this is that the person delivering the instruction assumes that the behaviour will occur as requested.

"Talking for a Purpose"

Now, if this assumption is supporting you to achieve the outcome that you want, do it. Keep that going. However, if you are not, I would like you to consider what are you actually thanking the child for?

Let us take this example: Sarah is in Year Two. She can be oppositional at times and does not always follow adults' instructions the first time. When given clear instructions she will often comply, after being given two to three reminders.

"Sarah, stand up and walk to the door, thank you." Yet Sarah has not actually moved. She is still sitting on her chair chatting to her friend Bethany about how her mum braided her hair this weekend. The teacher then says: *"Sarah and Bethany. I have already asked you. Now stand up and walk to the door, thank you."* Sarah is now chatting to Bethany about a birthday party, yet they are now standing up.

My question is, the thank you is reinforcing which behaviour?

As far as I can see; none…

So, if you are not getting the behaviour outcome and you are using thank you at the end of your sentence, take some time to stop and think what, are you actually thanking.

Ms. Morrish (MSc)

| CHAPTER ELEVEN |

The Drop and Stretch Technique

'I have been a teacher for 15 years and have attended many courses and read so many books on classroom management. Yet, for me, the 'Drop and Stretch' technique was a complete game changer in terms of being confident in managing ANY behaviour.'

Simon Sharpe, Year Five Teacher

By the end of this chapter, you will have a clear understanding of the following:

- ≈ Why the technique was developed.
- ≈ The significance of the Drop.
- ≈ The significance of the Stretch.
- ≈ The impact of Drop and Stretch within all learning environments.
- ≈ The significance of practising out of context.

What frequently happens, when faced with a challenging situation, adults' frequency of words and tone increases. As previously stated, when an adult or when a teacher is in a situation and they are expecting compliance, the rate of speech and frequency of words increase, leading to an increase in volume. Let us just take a moment to consider the children that you are verbally engaging with.

The majority of children often find themselves in situations where, let us be honest, adults are speaking to them at a high volume. Shouting possibly? They may be shouted at by their parents, or a higher level of volume by teaching staff because, what is often said to me is: I have to increase my volume in order to be heard.

Yet, this is what happens: the child that you are speaking to matches or increases the volume even more. Or they tune out completely. That is because the adult enters into a heightened state where they have a false belief that raised volume will equal being heard, when in fact, the opposite often occurs.

Why was the technique of Drop and Stretch Developed?

The technique of drop and stretch was developed as I want to give all educators a hands-on effective method that could be implemented immediately within all learning environments. I wanted to train all educators so that they experience an immediate increased behavioural compliance of children and supported adults to come out of their heightened state.

Part One: The 'Drop'

The first part is the Drop

The drop is simply as your tone increases, your depth of your sound decreases, so you sound deeper. The sound of your voice turns richer in sound. Just a slight variation in the tone increases the clarity of your words. Many teachers who implement the drop and stretch technique, often say, *'it is like that you sound like you mean, it without sounding mean.'* Therefore, sounding like you have more control of your words, with authority. The fantastic aspect of the drop, is that you only have to sound even the slightest bit deeper to have a positive effect on the clarity of your words.

Even if you are a female teacher who regards herself as having a high-pitched voice, you can still sound deeper, even if just slightly. Once you sound deeper, the children start to tune in or we can reframe that concept to attending and listening. They automatically start to attend to the sound and then the words and then both together. Another significant aspect to note is that, as previously stated, in my experience, once the adult drops, it is VERY difficult for the adult to re-enter into a heightened state.

Cortisol levels and adrenaline race through your body and when the drop happens, the fundamentals of how adults sound in control remain. You will sound like you have authority, and sound like you mean it <u>without</u> sounding mean, which is how you can develop positive relationships with the children in your class.

Ms. Morrish (MSc)

Part Two: The 'Stretch'

The second part is the Stretch

This simply means that you SLOW your words down and speak at a slower rate. I say to educators: *"If you think you are speaking slow, speak slower."* Speaking at a slower rate, automatically slows your words down and then stretches the words out. You again gain authority. You are not in a rush to say something. So again, you are gaining control and accountability for what you're saying. To reinforce, it is VERY difficult to enter back into a heightened state when you have slowed down your rate of speech.

Now, thanks to the slow rhythm of your words, children will, subconsciously, already be attentive and without question know that you are in control. A significant aspect in regards to the stretch is that both you and the child are given processing time. The child receiving the words is given the time and the space to process what is being said to them. Just by slowing your rate of speech down you will significantly increase the clarity of your behavioural instruction.

The Impact of Drop and Stretch within all Learning Environments

What the technique of drop and stretch consistently does is guide and structure you, so that you enter in a more resourceful state to deliver precise and clear behaviour expectations. This enables you to gain control of what you are saying; therefore, children receiving the information are in a much better position to process the information and then make a decision on what they are going to do, regarding their own behaviour.

"Ms. Morrish introduced me to 'Drop and Stretch'. This technique means your tension will not and cannot escalate and your blood pressure cannot rise. You remain calm and in control of your emotions and the power of a deep, slow voice means that the children are much more likely to respond with the outcome you are expecting. This not only changed my reaction within the classroom but also how I respond to my children at home."

Laura Turner, Year Two Teacher

Practising out of Context

It is imperative that you practise the drop and stretch technique out of context. The reason being, if you attempt this straight away within your classroom, without practise, may lead you into a heighten state. Also, as simple as this technique sounds; the feedback I have received from hundreds of educators, is that it is actually quite difficult to do!

Let us look at a non-classroom example first:

Ms. Morrish (MSc)

I didn't say you stole my money.

I didn't say you stole my money.

I didn't say you stole my money.

I didn't say you stole my money.

I didn't say you stole my money.

I didn't say you stole my money.

I didn't say you stole my money.

Now, drop and stretch on the words that are highlighted in yellow.

Now, write out a classroom instruction. For example,

Pencils down and eyes this way

Pencils down and eyes this way

Pencils down and eyes this way

Pencils down and eyes this way

Pencils down and eyes this way

Then highlight the words to be emphasised utilising the drop and stretch technique.

"Talking for a Purpose"

Reflective Questions:

Did you highlight the first word?

_____

Did you highlight more than one word?

_____

Did you highlight the word, and?

_____

Would you add in the child's name if this was an instruction for an individual child?

_____

What was the outcome just by changing the emphasis on the key words that you have chosen?

_____

Ms. Morrish (MSc)

"Talking for a Purpose"

|CHAPTER TWELVE|

The Impact of Changing Key Words for a Positive Behavioural Outcome

"I honestly never really considered how changing just a few words could have such a positive impact within the classroom.

I am not only conscious in terms of what I am going to say, but confident in how I say it"

Mr James Smith, Deputy Head Teacher

By the end of this chapter, you will have a clear understanding of the following:

- ≈ The significance of the word 'if' within a classroom setting.
- ≈ The impact of changing an 'if' to a 'when'.
- ≈ The impact of the word 'hope'.
- ≈ The impact if the word 'try'.
- ≈ Changing a 'but' to an 'and'.

Ms. Morrish (MSc)

The Significance of 'If' Within Classroom Settings

Let us consider the impact of changing some key words so you get a more positive behavioural outcome. One of the words that is stated frequently from educators is the word, *if*. Let us examine a non-classroom example first. Most people recognise and understand the importance of staying fit and healthy, particularly with regards to supporting an individual's positive mental health. It is considered that people also have gym memberships with the goal of increasing their cardiovascular capacity by getting fitter.

Therefore, a conditional sentence using this example would be something like, *"If I go to the gym, I will get fitter."* So, in this example, what is the significance of the word 'if'? It creates and presents a choice in a bi-directional communication. A choice has now been presented by the person communicating and the child receiving the information has now been given a choice. If you read the book, *"Talking for Purpose",* you will understand what a redundant question is. But you do have a choice, right? In fact, you do not have to read this book.

Now let us examine a classroom example. You are standing at the front of the class, delivering the learning objectives for the science session. Yet you are being interrupted by a few of the children who are talking amongst themselves. You feel that you have been clear with your language in regards to delivering the consequences for non-completed work.

You are confident that you have followed the steps clearly outlined in your school's behaviour policy, which states:

After you have given your three verbal warnings; please follow this script: *"If you don't finish your work, you can stay in at playtime to finish it."*

If the child continues to demonstrate 'low level disruption', he/she is to be kept in a break time to complete any work missed. Some children then think, *'I better finish my work, so I can go out to play'*, thus being able to think forward and make a prediction regarding their behaviour, so that they receive a positive consequence. Yet my central focus is upon children whose behaviour is viewed as more challenging, who hear that word *'if'* and it becomes a behavioural choice, which often results in a negative consequence such a missing playtime or minutes reduced off of Friday's reward time.

Reflective Task

Step one: Write out the following three examples and highlight the key words.

"If I don't go to the gym, I have wasted money on a non-used gym membership."

"If I choose not to continue to read the book, "Talking for Purpose", I will not understand what a redundant question is."

"If you don't finish your work, you can stay in at playtime to finish it."

Ms. Morrish (MSc)

During consultation with educators, I will often write out the adult's instructions, and then work in partnership to highlight the keywords that they are stating.

Did you highlight the same words as I did?

"If I don't go to the gym, I have wasted money on a non-used gym membership."

"If I choose not to continue to read the book, "Talking for Purpose", I will not understand what a redundant question is."

"If you don't finish your work, you can stay in at playtime to finish it."

Step Two: Have you noted any commonality at the end of each of these sentences?

'I have wasted money on a non-used gym membership' is a NEGATIVE OUTCOME

'I will not understand what a Redundant Question' is a NEGATIVE OUTCOME

"You can stay in at playtime to finish it."

"Talking for a Purpose"

Does this give you your positive behaviour outcome?

Step Three. Write out classroom examples that you have either said yourself or heard a colleague stating when the sentence started with an '*if*'. Then note whether the remainder of the sentence finished with a negative outcome.

Changing an 'If' to a 'When'

We have identified that the word '*if*' within a sentence provides a choice. However, what happens when you actually do not want to offer a choice to the child, you are giving the behavioural instruction to?

Now, replace the word '*if*' with '*when*'. Removing the '*if*' and replacing it with a '*when*' changes the whole impact of the sentence and its meaning. So, this is the only part within *"Talking for a Purpose"* that the person stating the sentence *assumes* that a positive behaviour will be the outcome.

Now, pay attention to the same sentences we wrote above, but this time we are going to change the '*if*' to '*when*'. *"When you have finished your work, you can go out to play."* The most noticeable difference is, upon replacing the '*if*' to a '*when*' the sentence finishes with a positive behaviour outcome, which supports adults to sound more confident with increased authority and clarity.

Let us go back to the gym example, *'when I go to the gym, I will get fitter.'* The statement, the processing of the words, the words and the whole process itself becomes your reality. Therefore, what you are stating becomes an action.

By you taking action increase your confidence and your accountability. Your thoughts become your behaviours; your behaviours become your actions. It is absolutely vital that you are crystal clear with what you are stating, because that will give you your behavioural outcome.

The word 'Try'

There is a famous quote regarding the word *'try'*, which some of you may already know. It comes from Yoda from Star Wars. Yoda's quote (picture above) succinctly sums up my personal thought process regarding the word *'try'*. What Yoda says is absolutely paramount. He states, *'Do or do not, there is no try'*. I am referring to the word *'try'*, so frequently stated by teachers in my tenure as a coach, consultant, and mentor.

As soon as someone uses *'try'* in a sentence, it makes me question their commitment. Think about it. What does the word *'try'* actually mean? For me, let us be honest, it means non-commitment.

It also possibly means lack of accountability, lack of confidence, and lack of being credible about what you are going to do. Because if you are going to *'try'* to do something, it is so unmeasurable and unspecific that it absolves any accountability.

Again, let us first take this concept out of the classroom. Here are some common situations when you may have used the word *'try'*.

- *"I'm going to try and drink less alcohol."*
- *"I'm going to try and eat less sugar."*
- *"I'm going to try and get up at 4am every day and go running, jogging or swimming."*

This is like a label and everyone comments, *"Oh! Well done, well done for trying."* My question is, *"Trying what exactly?"*

Just reframing it to simply *'I will'* or *'I am'* will increase your accountability and give you the opportunity for a positive behavioural outcome. The empowering statement changes your thought processes that lead to decisions and again, action.

Ms. Morrish (MSc)

When you say, *"I am going to try to do this,"* out loud; you have already told your brain that a little bit of effort is *okay*. You give yourself a buffer, yet it does not support you to move forward.

The lack of forward progression is primarily due to the fact that the little voice inside your head starts to speak. Then questions begin to be internalised and processed, such as, *"Why am I not losing any weight?"* or, *"Why am I being called into my head teacher's office?"* or, *"Why, am I not the leader in the field of this?"*

In fact, the statement that you are using, 'I'm going to try to do this,' is not benefiting you in any way. It is not helping you to move forward in your life, and it is not helping you to implement what you want to do.

With educators especially is, *"I'm going to try and implement "Talking for a Purpose", I'm going to try to deliver the consequences that are stated in my school's behaviour policy."* Or, *"I'm going to try to implement the behavioural system, I'm going to try to be on time, I'm going to try to do this, I'm going to try and present well at today's meeting."* The list is endless.

Practical Exercise

I am going to give you a practical exercise in order for you to gain greater insight. Place a pen, pencil, phone or TV remote control or whatever it is at hand right now in front of you. Here is my instruction. *"I want you to try and pick that up, I just want you to try."*

Of course, most of you **will** pick up the pen, pencil, remote control, but you are in no way **trying** to pick it up; either you have picked it up or you have not. You are not **trying** to attempt anything. You do it or you do not

Yoda is correct, *"YOU DO OR DO NOT, THERE IS NO TRY..."* It really is that simple.

The word 'Hope'

Another word to consider within your own language and the impact it has on your behaviour is the word *'hope'*. The word *'hope'* also means that you have a get out clause. To be clear, you are not taking ownership of your own language and behaviour. Again, there is no accountability, and trust me, the person hearing it really knows that you are not fully committed.

Let us examine the word 'hope'.

- *"I hope I can implement the behaviour management system in my new school."*
- *"I hope I can get to work on time."*
- *"I hope all of my children are going to follow instructions."*
- *"I hope everyone listens when I take assembly tomorrow."*

Ms. Morrish (MSc)

What happens with the word '*hope*' is you put yourself in a position of not being accountable. So how do we replace the word '*hope*' and increase your accountability? We replace the word '*hope*' with '*will*'.

- *"I will implement the behaviour management system in my new school."*
- *"I will get to work on time."*
- *"I will be clear and precise with my language so that the children are going to follow instructions."*
- *"Everyone will listen when I take assembly tomorrow."*

When I am consulting for schools, the minute somebody says that they are '*hoping*' or '*trying*', I virtually disregard it and know for a fact that it is probably not going to happen.

Some common uses of '*try*' I hear include, *"I will try to stop asking redundant questions."* Or *"I will try to manage my initial response."* Or *"I am just hoping that 'drop and stretch' actually works."*

What these questions do is encourage the person to introspect upon the impact their language has on their own behaviour. I support them to reframe their thought processes and to increase their accountability. Changing your language has a significant impact on **your** behavioural choices and decisions.

"Talking for a Purpose"

Reflective Activity

Practicing out of context

Step one: Become aware when you are talking to your family, your friends and your own children of how many times you actually say the word '*try*' and/or '*hope*'.

Step two: Be completely 100% honest with yourself. Did you really believe that you would follow through with what you said, when '*try*' and or '*hope'* was said?

_____

When you said the sentence, did you know consciously that you may not feel confident doing it?

_____

Alternatively, was it perhaps because you were not truly invested in your own words?

Step three: Empower yourself by changing your language. I challenge you to take out the words '*try*' and '*hope*' when you are speaking to anyone, not just the children in your classroom. Then note the impact: you will be surprised.

Ms. Morrish (MSc)

Changing a 'but' to an 'and'

The word *'but'* is far more powerful than you would imagine for a simple three-lettered word. It is often viewed as a word that can alter a person's option.

- *"That's a lovely dress you're wearing ... 'but'..."*
- *"You did a wonderful job with this...'but'..."*
- *"I like the first part of your presentation...'but'..."*
- *"Your spelling is really good... 'but' ..."*

What happens in your mind when a person says *'but'* after giving you positive affirmation, even before they say anything else? Think about a time when you received feedback regarding your ability to manage children's behaviour in your classroom. The feedback could have been from a mentor, work colleague or head teacher. Were you given positive affirmation followed by a *'but'*? What do you remember and how did this impact your classroom management in the future?

We respond emotionally by ignoring everything that was said before the *'but'* and focusing on what comes after it. Instinctively, we recognise that this is what they really think, feel or intend. The word *'but'* negates or cancels everything that goes before it. It is generally viewed as a signal that the actual important part of the sentence is coming up.

"Talking for a Purpose"

When you use the word '*but*', most people listening to you will give more attention and more weight to what you say after. This tiny little word is widely misused within educational settings.

If I said to you, *"my teaching assistant is really effective when working with small groups, but he really lacks presence in the classroom"* what would be your thoughts? Where would your focus shift in this sentence?

What if I were, to say to you, *"my teaching assistant is really effective when working with small groups, and he is really working on his presence in the classroom"* have your initial thoughts now changed?

Reflective Activity

Try this exercise with a friend. One of you begins a conversation with a sentence about anything. The second person adds a sentence of their own but starts with the word '*but*'. Continue talking for several sentences each but make sure that each sentence starts with '*but*'. Now try the exercise a second time but instead of starting the second and succeeding sentences with the word '*but*' use the word '*and*' instead and consider how much different you feel about it. Note how you feel when using different words.

Let us now examine some classroom examples:

Ms. Morrish (MSc)

Fill in the missing blanks:

I can see how hard you have worked today on your handwriting but/ and

_____

You're singing today during assembly was great but/and

_____

I really like how you helped your reading partner during paired reading but/and

_____

Change the words and note the positive impact upon children's behaviour, just by changing some key words.

|CHAPTER THIRTEEEN|

Choosing not to Attend

'When our school introduced Choosing Not to Attend. Myself and many others just thought, oh come on. It's just the same as tactical ignoring with a new fancy name. How wrong we all were.'

Trish Collis, Assistant SENCO

By the end of this chapter, you will have a clear understanding of the following:

- ≈ How the concept of choosing not to Attend evolved.
- ≈ The concept of tactical ignoring.
- ≈ The difference between Choosing not to Attend and tactical ignoring.
- ≈ The positive impact that Choosing not to Attend has within learning environments.
- ≈ The positive impact that choosing not to attend has for adults, who work on a 1-2-1 basis with children whose behaviour may be most challenging.

The previous chapter examined and discussed the importance of changing key words within statements and sentences which have a powerful impact on the behaviour and decisions that both you and the children are going to make.

However, there is also one significant key sentence that I hear often many times in schools. I have spent so many years wondering why adults are setting themselves up to do something they are actually unable to truly do. I know that some of you reading this may not fully agree with my personal thought process regarding the concept of *'ignoring'*.

There is a key phrase within *"Talking for a Purpose"* that is used in schools, which is called choosing not to attend. I am going to explain the difference between choosing not to attend and what is very, commonly stated and implemented within educational settings, which is called tactical ignoring.

First let us examine a commonly used classroom approach referred to as tactical ignoring.

To illustrate the concept, I am going to use an excerpt from behaviour expert Dr Bill Rogers, who states that:

"In every class there are hundreds of incidences of what we might call challenging behaviour. Often, it is not those you confront which make the difference but those you ignore. Behaviour expert Dr Bill Rogers explains the virtues of 'tactical ignoring'.

'Tactical ignoring' is the teacher's conscious decision to ignore certain behaviour and keep the focus on the flow of the lesson, or on acknowledging and reinforcing good behaviour. For example, when a

child calls out, you ask them to put their hands up like the rest of the class. When you turn away you can see them muttering about what you asked them to do or rolling their eyes. Tactical ignoring is the best approach to these situations and avoid the least disruption to the flow of the lesson. Pupils' notice what the teacher does attend to, students who follow the rule, put their hand up and wait- and they often follow suit.

There are the primary behaviours which you must choose to recognise and deal with such as children calling out and causing disruption. Then there are secondary behaviours which are the irrelevant accessories, which often come with primary behaviours, for example the rolling of the eyes when the pupil is asked to do something. These secondary behaviours should be ignored, even though irritating they are not the primary behaviour which was first acknowledged."

(Dr Bill Rogers, 2 October, 2012

Ref, osiriseducational.co.uk)

I would like to offer my thoughts in regard to the above excerpt which will stimulate your own thinking. Consider the following questions:

Ms. Morrish (MSc)

1. Is asking a child to put their hand up like the rest of the class, attending or ignoring the calling out?

   _____

2. Is asking the child to put their hand up the exact moment behaviour to address the calling out?

   _____

3. What words would you add in order to get your desired behaviour outcome?

   _____

4. Should secondary behaviours be ignored?

   _____

5. What if the secondary behaviour is your behaviour button?

   _____

What are your thoughts regarding the above excerpt?

_____

_____

I have lost count of the number of times an adult has said something along the lines of *"Oh we are ignoring Stuart's silly behaviour, aren't we Stuart?"* Or *"I have been told just to ignore her when she acts up like this"* while staring at the child. Or *"Yes, Sarah has been interrupting my lesson this morning by constantly calling out, so we are now ignoring that behaviour, aren't we?"* while sighing to her classroom assistant, Mrs Forbes. With each of these situations and thousands more, the child is actually being attended to, either consciously or sub-consciously.

A frequent statement said during classroom coaching is this, *"Ms Morrish, I am ignoring the calling out."* Within that sentence itself, you are **attending** to the behaviour. Just through their own language, the adult is admitting that they are not 'ignoring' the calling out at all!

I examined this concept and I wanted to devise a different sentence, something that would give all adults a clear and consistent structure. It would give an adult permission to not set themselves up by using the word ignore. It is a simple and effective sentence to address; low level as well as moderate level behaviours. The ones that often push your behaviour button; the situations where the child is safe and you are also safe. It is not that you are not going to manage this situation. It is that you are not ready.

Even just using the word ignoring in the title of the intervention, is setting your brain up to ignore something, even if you are being tactical around that. Please know, I understand the concept around tactical ignoring and the concept of choosing your battles.

However, I still firmly believe that the words themselves set adults up because ignoring behaviour means that you are ignoring it, you have to ***ignore*** it. If you think back to early behavioural approaches, a behaviour that is not reinforced either positively or negatively, is therefore ignored. The behaviour then becomes extinct, so it stops occurring. The child stops calling out. However, you are teaching children and not rats or pigeons. I firmly believe that ignoring within a classroom environment, in a school environment, is virtually impossible.

I wanted to develop a support for all adults that would create a consistent sentence so that everyone would understand the different philosophies that still gave them the positive behavioural outcome they desired. The ultimate outcome for me is to empower you to be ready, to manage any behavioural situation that you encounter.

Choosing not to Attend

The foundations and core values of choosing not to attend were built as I wanted to support all adults with a key phrase that could be universally embedded in learning environments. This in turn gives adults <u>permission</u> to not engage in a situation with a behaviour that they felt were not in a resourceful state to manage effectively.

I wanted to create a consistent buffer and allow you time to stop and think before you speak. The 35 seconds, or the five minutes if need be. Once you choose to <u>attend</u> to the behaviour, you will be in a resourceful state, which will then support you to:

- Manage your initial response.
- Manage your secondary response.
- Know in advance the behavioural outcome you want to see and/ or hear.

- Know in advance what you are going to say and *how* you are going to say the words.
- Add a congruent physical gesture if required.

Reader, please note that I am not talking about not attending to high level dangerous behaviours here. I am not talking about children who remove themselves from school's premises or children on the roof of the school. Nor am I talking about children coming in school with knives or swearing at either adults or peers. These behaviours must be attended to immediately.

The Difference between Choosing Not to Attend and Tactical Ignoring

When you choose not to attend to the behavioural situation that you are experiencing, you are in complete control of yourself, of your behaviour, language and responses in order to get the behavioural outcome you desire. When you consider the concept of ignoring, it is not measurable. You do not have a clear outcome.

Through implementing the choosing not to attend approach, it immediately increases your accountability. You now have a consistent buffer which allows you time to settle yourself before you interact with a child. The interaction between yourself and the child is going to be much more positive, just from changing the language of the sentence.

Ms. Morrish (MSc)

Impact of Choosing not to Attend within schools

After graduating from university, I worked one-on-one with a child who had autism and displayed extremely challenging behaviours. She was in year four within a mainstream primary school. She was non-verbal and at times physically aggressive towards myself and her peers. We often found ourselves outside of the learning environment as her behaviour was so disruptive.

However, we formed a fantastic bond. I quickly learnt her triggers, started to understand her vocalisations, developed visual prompts. I attended several courses to learn as much as I could about autism. Daily there was a high frequency of challenging behaviours with this child. Therefore, on a daily basis, I would be approached by several members of staff who would try and 'intervene'.

I know that this was coming from a genuine supportive place, but it just did not help me or the child. What it did was increase confusion for all. I decided to address this at the next whole staff meeting. This was when I was starting out in my career, early twenties. My concerns were met with a lot of stares and not much support.

The chaos continued until one day. We were in the corridor and the child was being loud with her vocalisations and refusing to walk. It was clear to me that she did not want to leave the music room. Two adults came over and stated that she was disrupting their classes learning time.

One of the adults said abruptly *"I have experience with children with autism, let me just take her"*. To which is replied calmly yet firmly to the adult, *"I have got this."* To which the adult replied *"but do you?"* My response again was calm but firm *"I have got this."* I then defused the situation and we both returned to the learning environment. I decided to state the same response to the next adult, then the next for days and weeks, until the message started to get through to the other members of staff.

I then explained at another staff meeting that if I said *"I have got this"* I really did, yet if I said *"Can you support?"* then staff would know that *I* was in need. Even what could be considered the very beginning of my career in schools, I never changed those two phrases. I said the same thing, in the same way every time. At this time, I was fresh out of university. I had no understanding of the true significance of consistent adult language.

Yet, I knew that it most certainly made a significant impact on my own behaviour, the child's and the school staff. The phrase choosing not to attend has had a significant impact within school environments. On a personal note, I have particularly noticed this for those adults who work one-on-one with a child or small groups whose behaviour may be viewed as particularly challenging.

This is especially evident when the behaviour is occurring outside of the classroom. For example, a child is refusing to re-enter the classroom and is in the corridor or the child is refusing to come into school after the end of playtime. What happens often is, in my experience, other staff feel that the best thing to do at that moment is to engage. This could be to engage with the child or the adult, or sometimes both.

Ms. Morrish (MSc)

This support can often be enabling the behaviours of the child that you do not actually want to see, which can lead to manipulation. When the adult has been trained and supported to use the phrase choosing not to attend, I feel that this gives a very clear message that unless requested, other adults should not intervene.

By changing the mindset of the language for adults throughout school, it empowers and gives adults the opportunity to ensure that when they are going to intervene and when they are going to speak, it would be regulated, with a purposeful and with and a measured outcome.

> *"Working as a one-on-one, 'Choosing Not to Attend' is vitally important. Using my knowledge and understanding of the child I am working with gives me the insight into knowing when they need time and space to calm down and process how they are feeling.*
>
> *I then make a judgement based on what I know and respond, or re-engage as and when I feel it is appropriate. Other staff allowing me to do this and not attempting to intervene is very important to how the situation can be resolved."*
>
> **Mrs Rogers, Behaviour Support Assistant.**

CHAPTER FOURTEEN

The Effective Commands Model

'As an NQT, I constantly thought, why don't my children follow instructions the first time. Then I realised that I was not implementing the MB's within the Effective Commands Model. I changed MY classroom behaviours which of course then helped to improve the children's behaviour.'

Mr Harrington, Year Three Teacher - NQT

By the end of this chapter, you will have a clear understanding of the following:

- ≈ The rationale of why the effective commands model was developed.
- ≈ What is meant by the term MBs?
- ≈ The four adult behaviours that increase when delivering an effective command.
- ≈ The one adult behaviour that decreases when delivering an effective command.
- ≈ The significance of being congruent.
- ≈ The mirror activity.

Ms. Morrish (MSc)

When in consultation with all education staff, no matter what age the children are, I constantly hear a response to this question, *"Tell me right now, what is your biggest concern?"* The answer is often a repetition of, *"He/she/they just never listen!"*

I wanted to develop a model for all educators to show how teaching staff can deliver effective commands and effective behavioural instructions. I have spent over fifteen years figuring this one out, looking to find some real, measurable and observable elements that could be presented as a model and can be utilised within any educational setting, for any child and any adult.

There are four adult behaviours that increase and there is one that decreases when delivering an effective behaviour command. These are known as the MBs.

Effective Commands Model – The MB's

Let us first examine the four adult behaviours that increase when delivering an effective command. Please note that you are not required to always implement all four MBs each and every time to state a behaviour instruction.

Therefore, depending on the situation, if you can only implement two, that is fine. However, if you are not seeing an increase in your children's compliant behaviours, it may be because you have not implemented one of the MBs. Also, upon first reading about the model for effective commands, it may sound too basic and simple. Yet, MBs are regularly not utilised either correctly individually or as a unit. As simple as the model may appear, educators often find it difficult to implement consistently.

Reader, please note, although the MBs are numbered, they are actually not designed to be put to use in any particular order.

The Four that Increase:
MB 1- Eye Contact

The first MB is eye contact.

Why is eye contact so significant when delivering an effective command? For making contact and communicating with a person, effective eye contact is essential in our everyday interaction with people, and also to those who want to be effective communicators.

Eye contact has a positive impact on the retention and recall of information and may promote more efficient learning as well as providing information about the target of others' expressions and cues about their communicative intentions and future behaviour (Baron-Cohen, 1995).

Eye contact and facial expressions provide important social and emotional information. People, perhaps without consciously doing

Ms. Morrish (MSc)

so, search other's eyes and faces for positive or negative mood signs. In some contexts, the meeting of eyes rouses strong emotions.

Eye contact provides some of the strongest emotions during a social conversation. This primarily is because it provides details on emotions and intentions. In a group, if eye contact is not inclusive of a certain individual it can make that individual feel left out, while on the other hand prolonged eye contact can tell someone you are interested in what they have to say. ("*Scientific American Mind*". *Scientific American Mind*. **27**: 8 and 9. Jan–Feb 2016)

I would just want to highlight that gaining and then maintaining eye contact is not for all children. So, for some children who may be a little bit anxious in a classroom or a child who has ASD, eye contact may not be appropriate.

However, if you feel that eye contact is appropriate in that moment, with that individual, then there is an increased opportunity for behavioural compliance. Eye contact from an adult also sends a message to the child that he or she are important.

Reflective Questions

1. How do you gain eye contact for your whole class?

___

"Talking for a Purpose"

2. How do you gain eye contact for an individual?

   _____

3. When is eye contact not appropriate?

   _____

4. How could gaining eye contact, be possibly linked to the concept of stopping the current behaviour first.

   _____

   _____

   _____

MB 2—Body Language/posture

The second MB - body language/posture

Why is body language/posture so significant when delivering an effective command?

Your presence within the classroom is often linked with your posture. Postures can have an effect on your ability to successfully manage challenging behaviour. The posture you adopt can have an impact on your voice as well. Therefore, I suggest you adopt a relaxed and upright posture to aid your vocal delivery.

Body language is something that is quite often discussed in regards to the teacher's presence within the classroom. I do not mean an adult standing over children. It is about everyone having the correct posture in the classroom. Most of the time you spend in the classroom you are actually standing up. Having a positive, authoritative and confident body language is very important when delivering a behavioural command.

Reflective Questions

1. What message do you think the children within your classroom receive via your body language?

   _____

2. Can you think of a person outside of education that you feel demonstrates confidence just because of his or her positive body language?

   _____

MB—3 Tone of Voice

The third aspect is your tone of voice, as explained within chapter eleven which describes the 'drop and stretch' technique. Again, to reiterate, the deeper you sound and the slower you speak, supports you to remain in a resourceful state.

This in turn increases the likelihood that the behavioural command will be complied with, resulting in a positive outcome for both you and the child.

Reflective Questions

1. Have you practised the 'drop and stretch' technique out of context?

2. What did you notice about the person receiving the information?

3. What did you notice about yourself as the communicator?

Ms. Morrish (MSc)

MB—4 Proximity

Finally, the fourth aspect is proximity. I often hear teaching staff saying, *"Ahh, but I can't walk around the classroom all the time to deliver the individual command, right?"* But you can increase your proximity, even with one or two steps, half a step sometimes, your proximity has increased. It is really important to think about proximity in terms of what it can actually give you and the children that you teach.

Here are just a few examples. It can stop some children being embarrassed, if a behaviour redirection is delivered across the classroom. It also increases your opportunity to feel differently if you feel that you are not going to be heard. It stops the repetition and also, it is very individualised. Increasing your proximity should actually be happening all the time due to you being an engaging and interactive teacher! Proximity control will happen naturally. Within your teaching style, moving around the classroom is vital, you can stand up in front of the classroom and teach. Increasing your proximity just slightly with authority is important.

Another strength of proximity is that it gives you that element of 'space' to stop and think before you speak. Just by increasing your proximity, interestingly, you are able to take the time and utilise your self-evaluating questions, thus enabling you to regulate so that you know what to say before you say it. Another significant aspect of increasing your proximity is directly linked to stopping the current behaviour first. There are some children in your classroom that possibly just need a physical prompt or gesture. You may have some children who do not respond as well to a verbal redirection given across the classroom as this may in fact be a negative trigger for some.

By increasing your proximity, you will be able to gesture that the pen goes down into the table, the chair legs become flat on the floor. The calling out stops and the silence happens because you have managed the space and the importance of proximity within the classroom. Remember to be congruent with your words and body and utilise open hand gestures

Reflective Questions

1. How do you manage proximity within your classroom?

   _____

   _____

2. Has increasing your proximity helped you to increase the clarity of your behaviour instructions?

   _____

Ms. Morrish (MSc)

3. Do you feel that by increasing your proximity, helps to support pupils who have additional needs?

One that Decreases – Sentence Length

Within the effective commands model, there is only one aspect that decreases. Before we explore what decreases, let us consider first, why this needs to decrease and not increase.

Think about a time where you have been in a situation and you are managing your classroom and feel you are not being heard. Or think about a time when you are talking to a table of children, just in a small group, and you give a behaviour instruction for everyone to look at you and listen.

Yet most children do not follow your instruction. Think about a time when you might be talking to a colleague about how to plan the Maths starter for tomorrow and it just was not completed in the way that you clearly explained.

What happens when you think or feel that you are not being heard or listened to? Well as previously discussed, you will go into what is called a 'heightened state'. As you now know, when you are in a 'heightened state', there are a few things that actually increase. One is your inability to stop and think before you speak.

Your rate of speech also increases. Yet what is the aspect that also increases during this time? Have you ever heard yourself saying, *"Why do I have to say this again?"* and *"Are you not listening?"* or *"Do I have to repeat myself to give this command?"* as well as, *"Why don't you do it the first time?"* Of course, you now know that these are possible, redundant questions yet why the need to add in extra words?

This has to do with your sentence length. It's a really interesting aspect. I hear this every single day. For some reason, as humans, as adults, if we feel that we are not being heard, the best solution is to add in more words!

For over twenty years, I have recorded the average sentence length in primary schools. On average, it is eight-ten words, sometimes more.

Here are some examples:

- *"I would like everyone to stand up and walk quietly to the carpet."*
- *"Jack, please stop calling out and raise your hand if you have something to say."*
- *"I would like to remind everyone of our class rules about kind hands."*

Let us take a moment just think about this developmentally. How many words are the children in your classroom actually processing? You give a command or behaviour instruction of *"Everybody stand

Ms. Morrish (MSc)

up and come and sit on the carpet." 10 words. Let us suggest that some children are hearing all of the words, processing the words and then following the instructions.

Some children may not be able to process all ten words, filter out a few and only process six words, some may only be capable of four. I then hear the adult saying, *"I have asked you all to come and sit on the carpet."* What in fact the adult has done is add in another six words which the child now also has to process and comply with. You could have 75%-80% of the children within your classroom processing your words and being compliant with your instructions. However, the other 20%, maybe 10%, maybe 5%, who are not processing your words.

What I really suggest is that instead of increasing your number of words, particularly if you feel frustrated, or you're not being heard, is actually to **reduce** your number of words. People often state less is more. I completely agree, particularly in reference to delivering effective commands.

Here is a classroom example:

Brenda is a seven-year-old girl. Although not considered to be a challenging child, has difficulty staying focused on her work without distracting others. She also struggles to follow adults' instructions the first time.

Her teacher Mr Byron asks, *"Brenda, please bring me your science book, so I can mark your work from yesterday afternoon."*

What words could be removed from the above sentence to support Brenda's ability to process this instruction? In this example the outcome is for Brenda to simply take her science book to her teacher. Therefore, I would remove the following words:

"Brenda, please bring me your science book. ~~So, I can mark your work from yesterday afternoon.~~*"*

Once Brenda has complied this the instruction, if you then feel it is necessary to state, *"So I can mark your work from yesterday afternoon"* please do so. Just by breaking down a 16-word sentence into two much shorter sentences, supports Brenda to process the words and increases the opportunity for a positive behavioural choice.

Reflective Task

Step 1 Think about a time when you felt that you did not get the behavioural outcome that you wanted

Step 2 Write out the sentences that you stated when giving your behaviour instruction

_____

_____

Ms. Morrish (MSc)

Step 3 Count the words in the sentence and ask yourself if there are any words that could be removed

_____

Step 4 Highlight the key words that you want to emphasise in your behaviour instruction

_____

_____

Step 5 Use the drop and stretch technique on your key highlighted words

_____

_____

Step 6 Practise out of context, saying your behaviour instruction.

Step 7 What did you notice?

The Importance of being Congruent

'I honestly thought that I was being very clear with my behavioural instructions. I had no idea that many of my words often did not match my body until I attended a "Talking for a Purpose" training session. The very next day, I changed not only my words but also my gestures to match and what a difference!'

Mrs Johnson, Year Two Teaching Assistant

What is congruency?

Within a classroom environment, if your words and body language do not match, it sends a mixed message to the person receiving the information. Children particular may misunderstand what is actually being asked of them if the adults' words, tone and body does not 'match'.

Ms. Morrish (MSc)

Impact of Gestures upon Behaviour Compliance

You may find yourself using your body, particularly your hands, when teaching. However, do you use your hands effectively when delivering a behaviour instruction? We need to be mindful of the gestures that accompany our words so that they become congruent. Some gestures occur at an unconscious level and can give away our emotions. So, the first step is to actually increase our own awareness of how we use our hands when communicating.

To improve your speech, use your hands

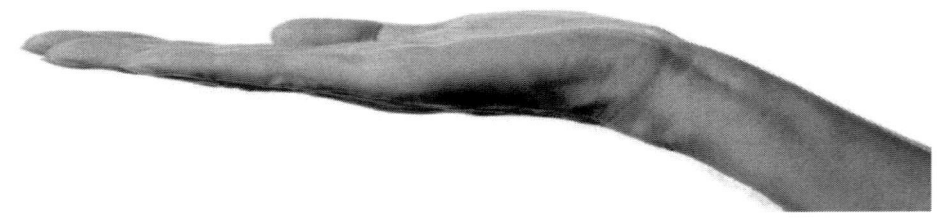

Carol Kinsey Goman, PhD (2019) is considered to be a world-wide expert in body language. In her article titled, Ten Powerful Body Language Tips, she sates:

"Brain imaging has shown that a region called Broca's area, which is important for speech production, is active not only when we're talking, but when we wave our hands. Since gesture is integrally linked to speech, gesturing as we talk can actually power up our thinking."

Ref:www.amanet.org/articles/10-powerful-body-language-tips

"Talking for a Purpose"

If you are incorporating hand gestures into your behavioural instructions, one tip I always encourage educators to do is to open their hands. This sends a much clearer message of what you actually want to see or hear. Experiment with this and you will find that the physical act of gesturing helps you form clearer thoughts and speak in a clear and precise manner.

Reflective Activity

Watch videos of famous speeches from anyone from Barrack Obama to The Queen and instead of listening to the speech focus on the speaker's body language. Turn the sound off for a few minutes.

When you turn it back on again, notice how speech and movement combine to create the whole impression.

As motivational speaker and author, Brian Tracey states:

"Your choice of words is important, but even more important is your tone of voice and your body language. However, the better you can coordinate all three of those ingredients, the more impact your message will have, and the greater the likelihood that a person will both understand it and react the way you want him to."

Brian Tracy (2019)

Ref: milled.com/brian-tracy/the-3-elements-of-communication

Ms. Morrish (MSc)

Mirror Activity

There is an activity that I often talk to my educators about, particularly in reference to delivering an effective command. One of the things that I strongly suggest is being videoed within classrooms. However, you may find that a little daunting.

As stated throughout this book, practicing out of context is vital. Here is an activity for you to practice out of context. Now initially, this probably sounds a little bit silly. However, for those of you that live with children, animals, partners, parents, grandparents and even if you live by yourself, one of the times that you *possibly* have the opportunity to be on your own, is in the bathroom.

I know it sounds a little bit obscure. However, this is my challenge to you. Here is your activity, from Monday to Friday, when you are in the bathroom in the morning, getting ready for work, getting ready to go to school or getting ready to take your children to their school. Give yourself a behaviour command and look in the mirror. Yes, it is going to feel weird. All I want you to do is say five times the same command, such as *"Pass me the shower gel."* or, *"Turn the hot tap off."* Or, *"Let me plug in the hair straighteners."* Or, *"Plug in the hair straighteners."* Whatever you choose to say, give yourself a behavioural command.

And yes, you are going to feel very silly. Possibly some people in your household are going to wonder what is going on!

1) Give yourself a behaviour command, five times each morning and evening. (5 days)

2) Give yourself a different behaviour command. This focusing on using the drop and stretch technique. five times each morning and evening. (5 days)
3) You can again keep the same command or change it for week three.

I am only asking for 15 days. By the end of the 15 days, you would have relaxed and delivering the command becomes a habit. That is what the children in your class are seeing and hearing. What happens with this is that once relaxed, you will sub-consciously revert back to your 'default behaviour.' You may need to persevere.

Your self-reflective questions could include:
1. Am I too near or far away from the mirror?
2. Do I turn away when speaking?
3. Are my words clear and precise?
4. Is my rate of speech too fast? Too slow?
5. I am using the drop and stretch technique on the words I want to emphasise?
6. Am I talking too much?
7. Are my words and my body congruent?

This is a brilliant platform for you to be able to introspect and where necessary, change your behaviour. Change how you look and also change how you sound. I challenge you to do this short yet effective task. Your ability to change your behaviour, language and responses will be vital within any classroom, and for any year group that you will teach throughout your career.

Ms. Morrish (MSc)

|CONCLUSION|

"We have implemented "Talking for a Purpose" within our school for the past nine years. Due to the consistency of the adult's language, "Talking for a Purpose" provides time and recognition that creates a platform for the development of positive relationships between ALL adults and ALL children."

Mr Mike Wood, Head Teacher

"Talking for a Purpose" has been successfully implemented in many, many schools. Head teacher, Mr Mike Wood and others firmly believe that it has built a healthier learning environment where the relationships between the adults and children have improved significantly. I also believe that by implementing this approach there is a significant increase in on task behaviour and behavioural compliance which ultimately equates to even more teaching time.

This approach has been in development now for over 20 years, thousands of educators have received *"Talking for a Purpose"* training and my aim is for hundreds of thousands more to be able to access this training.

Just to recap, the benefits it will have on the adult and children are profound. Namely but not limited to:

- Increased accountability of adults' behaviour
- Empowering adults to make positive choices

Ms. Morrish (MSc)

- Increased teaching time
- Increased adult self-regulation
- Increased positive mental health for all
- Providing a basis of correct language at the right time in the right place
- Children benefiting from consistency
- Increased attachment behaviours
- Lower frequency of all level of behaviours
- Reduction in the rate of exclusions

It is important to note that *"Talking for a Purpose"* is not solely exclusive to a classroom or a school setting. There will be aspects and concepts in this book that will spill over and enrich your day-to-day life.

My final piece of advice for you; is to always;

Say What You Mean and Mean What You Say.

MS. MORRISH (MSc)

Independent Behaviour Consultant

"Talking for a Purpose"

|Me, in my oversized school blazer|

Ms Morrish is available for full day and half day CPDS and INSET trainings, for *"Talking for a Purpose."* If you also feel that your school would benefit from Ms Morrish's personal classroom coaching, please contact:

pachangebehaviour@gmail.com

Or

Ms Morrish on: msmorrish@changebehaviour.co.uk

For social media please follow:

Facebook – ChangeBehaviour@msmorrish

Instagram – changebehaviour_1

Ms. Morrish (MSc)

FEEDBACK

"Talking for a purpose" has a significant impact on the way the staff are speaking to the children, which instantly changed the way the children responded and behaved. It made the whole school feel more positive, staff more confident and the consistency was reassuring to the children."

Mrs Walla,

SENCO and Deputy Head teacher

"Talking for a Purpose" has empowered our staff to take 'back control'. This has resulted in significant improvements in children's behaviour that is commented upon by everyone that now visits our school."

Mrs Debbing,

SENCO

Ms. Morrish (MSc)

"Talking for a Purpose allowed me to feel more in control of any behaviour situation. I felt a huge increase in my confidence as a teacher. All aspects of "Talking for a Purpose" has helped me to flourish as a teacher."

Ms Nizami,

Year Six Teacher

"In Baltimore, we have sustained many of the elements of the program and lessons from Ms Morrish in our early childhood mental health consultation projects. Her proactive approach taught us how to be "ready" for challenges so that we could empower teachers, parents and students to be prepared to work through challenging and difficult incidents as well as sensitive situations."

Kay Connors,

Program Director of

University of Maryland, Baltimore

"Talking for a Purpose"

"Ms Morrish is THE most influential person I have met on my teaching journey, hands down. Wonderful to have her in the education industry."

Mrs Gwen,

Trainee Teacher

"The techniques in "Talking for a Purpose" provide the foundation of my day-to-day classroom management. Implementation is simple and the adult-led methods provide immediate, sustainable results. There will always be a copy on my bookshelf!"

Mr H McLeod,

Year Six Teacher and Computing lead

Ms. Morrish (MSc)

|INDEX|

"

"Talking for a Purpose", 3, 16, 67, 99, 115, 134, 137, 146, 169, 175, 176

B

Behaviour, 3, 15, 16, 65, 66, 67, 68, 73, 74, 75, 76, 83, 84, 85, 86, 105, 106, 107, 108, 109, 110, 111, 113, 114, 115, 116, 117, 118, 119, 120, 124, 131, 133, 134, 137, 138, 139, 141, 143, 146, 147, 148, 149, 150, 151, 152, 153, 155, 156, 157, 159, 162, 163, 164, 165, 167, 168, 169, 172, 173, 175
Behavioural compliance, 74, 122, 158, 175

C

Challenging behaviours, 152
Classroom management, 16, 76, 99, 141
Congruency, 169
Current behaviour, 115, 116

D

Defiance, 65
Disruption, 131

Drop and stretch, 121, 122, 124, 125

E

EMB, 105, 108, 111, 112, 113, 114, 117
Exact moment behaviour, 105, 108, 109
Exact moment behaviours, 108
Executive head teachers, 75
Eye contact, 157

H

Head teacher, 78, 90, 136, 141, 175
Heightened state, 73, 76, 79, 90

I

Independent Behaviour Consultant, 1, 176

L

Language, 3, 16, 64, 66, 67, 76, 103, 115, 118, 119, 130, 138, 139, 140, 149, 151, 152, 153, 154, 159, 160, 169, 170, 171, 173, 176, 185

M

Managing state model, 73, 79, 85
Mirror activity, 172

N

NQTs, 75

O

Out of context, 66, 67, 103, 125

P

Perceived behaviour, 105, 106
Posture, 81, 82, 83, 159, 160
Practising out of context, 80, 121
Presenting behaviour, 117
Primary school, 152

R

Rate of speech, 85
Redundant question, 87, 88, 95, 97, 133
Redundant questions, 87, 90, 91, 93, 105, 111
Redundant statement, 99
Reflective questions, 127, 158, 160, 161, 163
Reflective task, 131, 167
Regulated breathing, 71, 79

S

School administration personnel, 75
Secondary school, 91
Self-evaluating, 88, 96, 97, 105, 113, 114, 162
Self-Evaluating question, 96
Senior teachers, 75
Stress hormone, 78

T

Tactical ignoring, 145, 146, 147, 149
Teacher's presence, 159
The significance regarding the word 'Sometimes', 97
Think BEFORE you speak, 69
Tone, 122, 123, 160, 169, 171
Trainee teachers, 75

Book References

Branden, N. (1994). The six pillars of self-esteem. New York ; London: Bantam

Brian Tracy, (2019) Ref: milled.com/brian-tracy/the-3-elements-of-communication

Carol Kinsey Goman, PhD (2019) Ref: www.amanet.org. (n.d.). 10 Powerful Body Language Tips. [online] Available at:

http://www.amanet.org/articles/10-powerful-body-language-tips

David Harold Hargreaves, Hester, S.K. and Mellor, F.J. (1975). Deviance in classrooms

Dr Bill Rogers, 2 October, 2012 Osiris Educational. (n.d.). Osiris Educational - Home | Training for Teachers | Online CPD. [online] Available at: http://osiriseducational.co.uk

Fullan, M and Hargreaves, A., (ed.) (1996) in Teacher Development and Educational Change, *Teacher Development and Educational Change* pg. 1   The Falmer Press, London (1996)

Gideon O. Burton, Brigham Young University. Rhetorical questions!" specialized language definitions. Archived from

http://rhetoric.byu.edu/figures/R/rhetorical%20questions.htm

Haralambos and Holborn (2013) Sociology Themes and Perspectives. Journal of Personality and Social Psychology. **6** (1): 109–114.

Mindblindness: An Essay on Autism and Theory of Mind. By S. Baron-Cohen. (Pp. 168; £17.95.) MIT Press: Cambridge, Mass. 1995. Psychological Medicine, 28(3), pp.743–749

Rist, R. (1970). Student Social Class and Teacher Expectations: The Self-Fulfilling Prophecy in Ghetto Education. Harvard Educational Review, 40(3), pp.411–451.

Rosenthal, R. and Jacobson, L. (1968). Pygmalion in the classroom : teacher expectation and pupils' intellectual development. New York Etc.: Holt, Rinehart And Winston.

Shirley Ann Millard (1999). Mr Toad gets the silent treatment. Ilfracombe: Arthur H. Stockwell.

Trimboli, A. & Walker, Michael B. (1987) Non-verbal dominance in the communication of affect: A myth? Journal of Non-verbal Behaviour. 11, 180-190.

Printed in Great Britain
by Amazon